Hear me carefully

John Blanchard is a man of God. He is a man who walks with God, who knows God, and has a deep and passionate love for the Son of God. He has a burning desire to proclaim the gospel of Christ to the nations of the earth. John has filled the earth with the knowledge of the Lord. His writings, books and pamphlets have been published in many languages, and it is true to say that this man of God is loved by the church in nearly every land. John's ministry of apologetics has been used of the Lord to defend the faith and to proclaim the gospel of saving grace.

John Blanchard is a special gift from the Lord to his church. In every age there are those who, by the sovereign grace of God, stand head and shoulders above the rest because they are so gifted, so unique, and so used of the Lord.

John is one of those and this is his amazing story.

Pastor Robert L. Dickie
Berean Baptist Church, Grand Blanc, Michigan

Reading through this book, *Hear Me Carefully*, transported me instantly back to so many remembrances of sitting under the faithful ministry of John Blanchard. Over the course of four decades, since I was a teen, I have had the privilege of hearing him preach. I love the clarity and simplicity and boldness of his messages. I love the care and propriety with which he composes and deploys turns of phrases that arrest the hearers' attention and drive deep truths home to the heart. I love benefiting from the fruit of his voracious reading and his gleanings from the best of Christian literature. So I want to commend this brief record of John's rich and long ministry to you. You will read it with edification. It is the story of our great God choosing a humble gospel servant and giving him a wide ministry and going before him every step of the way.

Senior Minister, First Presbyterian Church, Jackson, USA
Professor of Systematic and Historical Theology, RTS
President, Alliance of Confessing Evangelicals

No one in our generation has done more than John Blanchard to explain the gospel with winsome clarity and biblical accuracy. He has a wonderful gift for communicating even the hardest biblical truths in simple terms — and he is driven by an inde-fatigable passion to rise above the silliness, anger, negativity, noise and shallowness of today's public discourse in order to tell people about Christ. The message to which John has devoted his life is the best possible Good News, and he communicates accordingly. The evangelistic tracts and booklets he has written are indispensable tools for today's church. They are some of the most lucid, persuasive, thorough, helpful gospel presentations available. We use them weekly in the ministries of Grace Community Church and The Masters College.

Evangelistic zeal is delightfully contagious, and no one is more infectious than John Blanchard. I thank God for John's faithful-ness and his influence.

As this excellent biography reveals, there's a reason John Blanchard is so enthralled with the grace of God and so eager to proclaim the saving work of Christ. He himself was arrested by the truth of the gospel, transformed by the power of the Holy Spirit, and providentially directed into the ministry he has been devoted to for the past fifty years. The story of his life is an upbeat and uplifting celebration of God's work in a sinner's life, to the praise of God's glorious grace.

John MacArthur
Pastor, Grace Community Church, Sun Valley, California
President, The Masters College and Seminary, CA

HEAR ME CAREFULLY

JOHN BLANCHARD — A BIOGRAPHY

Marlene Williams

 BOOKS

EP Books
Faverdale North
Darlington
DL3 0PH, England

www.epbooks.org
sales@epbooks.org

EP BOOKS are distributed in the USA by:
JPL Distribution
3741 Linden Avenue Southeast
Grand Rapids, MI 49548

E-mail: orders@jpldistribution.com
Tel: 877.683.6935

First published 2012

British Library Cataloguing in Publication Data available
ISBN: 978 085234 785 0

To TGM
from The Mighty M.
What a privilege!

Contents

Preface

Those of you who are familiar with John Blanchard's preaching will recognize the title of this book. It is a phrase he uses frequently when addressing an audience. 'Hear me carefully...' is his repeated request to emphasize the importance of the message of the Christian gospel, which he has been bringing to countless people across the world for over fifty years.

This is not a story of John Blanchard's achievements, but of what God has done through him. It tells how God, in his goodness, took a nobody, from a tiny island in the English Channel, and used him beyond anything he could ever have imagined. It is a testimony to God's amazing provision and guidance in a life totally dedicated to him.

Marlene Williams

March 2012

1
Small beginnings

This story begins on the tiny island of Guernsey, which lies 100 miles off the south coast of England and thirty miles off the coast of Brittany in France. Guernsey, which measures only five miles by three, is one of the Channel Islands and, although loyal to the British Crown, is not part of the United Kingdom, but anyone born there is entitled to hold a British passport and to be known as 'a citizen of the United Kingdom, Islands and Colonies'. One of the island's main industries was, and still is, the production of thousands of tons of tomatoes in miles and miles of greenhouses. In the 1930s many islanders were employed as greenhouse labourers, working very hard for only a basic wage. One of those was Jack Blanchard, who lived with his young wife Ivy in St Sampson's.

On 10 July 1932 a baby boy was born to Jack and Ivy, who were then living in Castle View, Sampson's Harbour. His parents named him John William. About three years later a second boy, David, was born and that completed the family. They were not to know that their happiness would be short-lived. Two years later, in 1937, the little family was torn apart by the tragic death of Ivy. She was only twenty-four years old and died of ulcerative colitis, something easily curable these days.

To help with the care of his two boys, Jack arranged for the eldest son, John, to stay with 'Auntie May', who lived about two miles away in the northern part of the island. She was a generous, warm-hearted lady and under her loving care John felt the pain of losing his mother fade away. The little boy settled in well and it seemed the most natural thing in the world to go to Delancy Elim Church with her, where she was an enthusiastic member. He hardly missed attending a service and for the next three years his life was filled with pleasant, uneventful days.

Yet all too soon the family faced another crisis. In 1940 their peaceful island life was shattered by Adolf Hitler when his troops invaded and occupied the Channel Islands. News of the impending German invasion caused the Guernsey authorities to announce the evacuation of all schoolchildren. This had to be carried out within twenty-four hours and, with no time to think, Jack made a traumatic decision. The following day, 20 June 1940, his two small boys sailed from St Peter Port Harbour on SS *Felixstowe*, away from their beloved island home, each taking just a few personal belongings and a gas mask. They joined thousands of other children in a mass exodus leaving behind all ties to their homes and families.

Seven days later, the harbour was bombed and many people lost their lives. Two days after that, thousands of troops landed on the island. The German occupation had begun. Jack was now behind enemy lines and there was to be no communication between him and his two sons until the war ended in 1945.

Meanwhile, the two young boys were taken by boat to Weymouth and then by train to Scotland, where they joined many other evacuees. David was taken to live with a coal-mining couple in Shotts, a small town in the county of North Lanarkshire, while John was moved from one welfare centre to another before finally being shipped to an island off the west coast of Scotland. This was Islay, one of the islands of the Inner Hebrides, and it was 500 miles away from his home. The two brothers were now 100 miles apart and there was to be no further contact between them for the duration of the war.

John found himself on a working farm in the care of a middle-aged couple, John and Jessie MacGillivray. They had no children of their own and no parenting skills. For the next five years John lived a crude and simple life on an island that had more sheep than people and was a mixture of fertile farmland and bleak, lonely moors. He went about barefoot and was not allowed in the house until dusk. The fields became his playground and the farm implements his toys. A mixed collection of animals, including thirteen cats, became his friends. The islanders spoke Gaelic, and within a few months John was fluent in their native tongue. Despite being only eight years old, he was introduced to a daily work routine which included sowing and harvesting crops, milking, moving cattle, ploughing and also the back-breaking business of digging and cutting peat.

On 5 May 1941 he was enrolled in Newton of Kilmeny Primary School, and for the next two years he walked three miles to and from the school, often barefoot. The headmaster, Mr D. McLean, told Mrs MacGillivray that John had 'an intelligent forehead' and awarded him a prize for 'General Excellence'. John then graduated to Bowmore High School, which involved more walking and two bus rides. Life became an endless round of work and school. Although there were churches nearby, church attendance became a thing of the past and he gave no thought whatsoever to God.

In 1945, with the end of the war in sight, arrangements were made for the evacuees to return home. Through the Red Cross, permission was given for each child to receive a twenty-five-word telegram from their parents. John's telegram took him completely by surprise because it was signed, 'Your Mother-to-be'. He had no idea what this could mean until the MacGillivrays suggested that his father was planning to remarry. Faced with this and the prospect of leaving the rural life he had now become accustomed to, John ran away. He hid in the nearby hills to avoid the welfare agent who was sent to escort him to the mainland. A search party found him, and he was soon on his way to mainland Scotland, and from there to Weymouth by train. He then joined hundreds of other children in a school playground and waited for a ship to complete the final part of the journey. As he wandered around the playground, he noticed a boy sitting on a suitcase. He did not recognize the boy, but he certainly recognized the name on the luggage label — it was his brother David. So the two were reunited and were soon swapping stories.

Finally, on 6 September 1945, SS *Hantonia* sailed into the harbour of St Peter Port, bringing Guernsey's children home for an emotional reunion with their parents. John and David met the lady who was now their stepmother, and family life began again.

The Blanchard family lived in a first-floor flat with basic amenities, and for John this was a far cry from the freedom of a rural landscape. There was no electricity or running water (other than down the walls!) and all provisions such as coal and buckets of water had to be carried up two flights of stairs. Bath-time was once every two weeks, and John was always fourth in the queue to use the bathwater.

The new Mrs Phyllis Blanchard soon became 'Mum' and, as she was a regular churchgoer unlike their father, who never darkened the doors of a church, she quickly invited the boys to Holy Trinity Church. John, who had considered himself to be 'an independent, teenage heathen' on Islay, decided to see what it was like. There was little else to do on Guernsey, and so he joined the choir and then the Sunday School. He became a junior usher and later joined the Youth Fellowship, never missing a meeting or a practice. John says, 'I joined everything except the ladies' meeting — and that was only because I wasn't invited!' He went to a church camp and wrote a report for the parish magazine after which the vicar suggested, prophetically as it turned out, that he should try writing his own books. Throughout the next few years he became a good, religious boy.

He left school at sixteen years of age with no formal qualifications. In 1948 he joined the Guernsey Civil Service, working in the Greffe Public Record Office. He became a member of the St Peter Port Boxing Club, but eventually became tired of being used as a 'punchbag' and left the sport. In later years, when telling people about his boxing 'career', he often claimed to have met Muhammad Ali — before adding, 'It was outside the ring!'

John was adventurous by nature, and this had already put him in danger. As a child, he enjoyed going to the place where his father worked, but one day he climbed up the side of a huge water butt and fell in. He couldn't swim and screamed for help. Fortunately at that moment a workman was passing and saved the little boy from drowning. Now, as an older teenager, this adventurous spirit continued to put him at risk. One night he decided to go swimming with a friend, but in the darkness he underestimated the strength of the wind. At midnight, in rough seas off the cliffs on the island's south coast, John found himself alone and unable to swim any further. He was on the point of drowning when his screams were heard by his friend, who appeared out of the darkness just in time to bring him safely to the shore. He was also an intrepid climber and on another occasion he slipped while inching his way along a high cliff-face. Once more help was at hand, this time in the form of a small bush growing out of the rock which was just enough to save him from a fatal fall.

He continued to go to church and became a Sunday School teacher, after which he progressed to the role of Youth Leader. Church was the focal point of his life and, with his main interest being young people, he was a pastor's dream. He joined the National Association of Youth Clubs and in 1953 was elected chairman of the National Members' Council. John's church activities kept him very busy, but he had become something on the outside that he was not in fact on the inside, and he deceived many people as well as himself.

He started to play competitive snooker and won trophies at the Imperial Club, home to Guernsey's best players. He was chosen to play against the visiting Jack Rea, one of the world's leading professionals from Northern Ireland, and was expected to become the Channel Islands Champion. Yet it was this sport that slowly led him into smoking, drinking and gambling. It was usual for him to dash away from a Sunday morning church service, spend the afternoon gambling (often losing money) and then hurry back to teach his Sunday School class. In his own words, he became a 'full-blown hypocrite — Christianity was a performance, not an experience.'

2
Religion versus reality

In 1954 three things happened which were to have an enormous impact on John and would change the direction of his life for ever.

The first was the arrival of a new minister at his church. The Reverend Arthur Geary Stevens was a good sports-man who joined in all the young people's activities and was great fun to have around. However, it was his preaching that had the greatest impact on John. It was direct and challenging. This irritated John, who often felt that the sermons were directed at him and won-dered why the man seemed to know so much about him. He did not like the repeated question: 'Have you ever trusted Jesus Christ as your personal Saviour?' Despite growing unease, he maintained his role as Youth Leader and became involved in fund-raising for the South American Missionary Society. This did not fool Arthur Stevens, who soon began to have grave doubts about the reality of John's Christianity. Neither he nor John knew what was around the corner.

The second was the sighting of a blonde walking down Corfe Row, where she worked for the Attorney General. It was love at first sight. To John she was the most beautiful girl in the world, with a smile that could melt an iceberg, and he decided that she was the one he wanted to marry. A few months later, John was overjoyed when the Civil Service transferred him to the Attorney General's Office. At last he met the blonde and found out that her name was Joyce McKane. Better still, her desk was 'within perfume range' of his! However, the attraction was dampened when he realized that her conversation with another member of staff during every coffee break was always on the subject of church — what the preacher had said and how God was blessing his people through the preaching. While John was very religious on at least three days every week, this young lady went much further. He had enough religion when he was at church, especially on a Sunday, and did not see the need to talk about it on Monday. He decided she was a religious maniac and should be kept at arm's length. Yet the quality of her life told him that she had something he didn't have, and his attraction to her remained.

The third thing was an unexpected invitation from Joyce. She asked him if he would like to go to an evangelistic campaign to be held in Candie Gardens Auditorium, St Peter Port, from 10 to 24 October 1954. He flatly refused. Undeterred, she persisted in her request, telling him that he would enjoy hearing the speaker. The man's name was Paul Cantelon, a Canadian and a cousin of Walt Disney. He was a talented artist and painted a picture every night as well as speaking. Not even this could persuade John to go. Not to be outdone, the young lady tried one final approach. She told John that she was travelling to the venue every night by bus and he could meet her at the bus stop and go with her. Needless to say, he had a sudden change of mind and agreed to go.

He hated it. It was exactly as he had feared, 'too jazzed up and high powered'. He was used to a liturgical Church of England service and this was completely foreign to him. He listened to the preaching but decided he had heard it all before. Years of going to church had taught him all the facts about the Christian faith. Yet, rather annoyingly, the evangelist was endorsing everything his new minister had been saying.

But he continued to go — because Joyce was going. Despite his determination not to let it get to him, he felt as though the pieces of a jigsaw puzzle were starting to fit together in a very personal and uncomfortable way.

Slowly and reluctantly, John began to realize that this could revolutionize his whole life.

First of all, the preacher said that there was one true and living God who was sovereign, holy, eternal and all-powerful. He was the Creator of all things in the universe, known and unknown. John found that easy to accept.

Secondly, God created man in his own moral and spiritual image. Mankind was the crowning glory of his creation — highly sophisticated, intelligent, moral beings who delighted in obeying God. The first man, Adam, and his wife, Eve, lived in obedience to their Creator and enjoyed a close relationship with him and with each other on a perfect earth. Then something happened that was to have profound consequences which have lasted to this day. There came the moment when Adam broke God's law for the very first time and, in disobeying his Maker, he not only sinned but he became a sinner. From that moment everything was ruined. His relationship with God was shattered and he, who had been God's friend, became an enemy and a rebel.

John knew enough of the Bible to know that this was true, but it was the next bit that he found very difficult to accept. Adam then fathered children after his own fallen image, and we are part of that stream over the centuries. John was told that he was by nature defiled and godless, and that there was nothing he could do to put things right. Good works couldn't do it; kindness, helping others, fund-raising or religion — none of these could bridge the gap. Neither could church attendance, praying (which for him was minimal) or Bible study (which was absolutely zero in his case). This was the bit that irritated John the most. To be told that all his religious activities counted for nothing hit him hard. He had been christened as a baby, confirmed as a young teenager and was now a communicant member of the Church of England. Yet he was being told that none of this contributed to getting right with God. The more he heard it repeated night after night, the more it irritated him, and yet, somewhere deep inside, he started to see that it was true.

But the preacher had more to say. He had some good news. God, in his amazing love, had intervened in this desperate situation. He had come into the world himself, in the person of the Lord Jesus Christ, to save sinners. He had lived the perfect life that we could not live, and then died on a cross, taking upon himself the physical and spiritual death penalty that God prescribed for sinners. The Bible teaches that death is the result of sin, but here was a man with no sin, and yet he died. Paul Cantelon explained that Jesus Christ was made sin for us and took the punishment that was due to us. Yet three days later he rose from the dead and is

alive today. Because of this he is able to offer forgiveness of sin and eternal life to all who would abandon
not only their wickedness, but also the good bits of
their lives, their religion and their version of Christianity, and fling themselves utterly on Jesus Christ.

John had never seen the truth so clearly or completely.
He suddenly felt as though he had found something he
had missed for years. Finally, the last piece of the
jigsaw puzzle fell into place. That night, at the end of
the service, the congregation sang a well-known hymn
by Fanny Crosby:

> Pass me not, o gentle Saviour,
> Hear my humble cry,
> While on others you are calling,
> Do not pass me by.

John sang the first verse as a religious hypocrite. He
sang the last verse as a converted Christian. When he
sang the words he meant them with all his heart. God
heard him and did something amazing, convincing and
lasting. He brought John into a living relationship with
himself.

So, in October 1954, John Blanchard, long-time Sunday
School teacher and Youth Leader, became a Christian.
But what difference would this make to someone
already steeped in religious activities? The change was

immediate and very clear to John. He likened it to the signs of life in a newborn child: it cries out and it wants to feed. He immediately 'cried out', telling his minister first, and then anyone who would listen.

Later that week he decided to tell the members of his Youth Fellowship. The young people met every Thursday night to play games, and then to have what was laughingly called an epilogue. This consisted of a hymn and then a prayer which John read from a book. The next Thursday was quite different. Instead of reading the usual prayer, John read the story of Paul's conversion from Acts chapter 9. He then shared his own story with them, telling them of their need to trust in Jesus as Saviour.

He also experienced a great hunger for God's Word and wanted to feed on its teachings. The only Christian broadcasts were from Radio Luxembourg. John waited each night until his parents were in bed and then turned on the radio very low so as not to disturb them. He listened to anybody who was talking about the Bible and about Jesus Christ. He enjoyed the teaching from programmes such as *The Old-Fashioned Revival Hour* with Charles E. Fuller from Long Beach, California. He read his Bible daily and devoured its message, wanting to know more and more about his Saviour. These were instant signs of new life in the once religious Youth Leader, and John knew that an encounter with God had made all the difference. His passion for evangelism grew, and he was determined to devote his whole life to sharing the good news of the gospel with others.

Not only did he grow as a Christian, but he also fell deeply in love with the young lady who had persuaded him to attend the event that changed his life. Now a fervent Christian, John could share with Joyce the most important and precious thing in both their lives — their faith and trust in Jesus Christ. Under God's guiding hand, their relationship grew, and three years later they decided to get married. They wrote their own wedding service, which included the singing of a suitable psalm. However, John's grasp of Roman numerals in his Bible left a lot to be desired and he gave the printer the wrong psalm. When the order-of-service leaflets were delivered the psalm to be sung was the one which said, 'God be merciful to me … until these calamities be overpast.' Fortunately there was enough time to correct the mistake, and they were married on 22 August 1957 at Holy Trinity Church, Guernsey, where Joyce then joined him in active Christian service. John had no idea what God had in store for them, nor did he realize the vital role Joyce was to play in selflessly enabling him to follow God's plan for his life.

In 1960 he was licensed by the Bishop of Winchester as a Lay Reader in the Church of England. He was required to read the lesson in Holy Trinity Church and took this extremely seriously. He set high standards for himself and practised reading for hours in the bedroom, often staining his shirt with perspiration from the effort. He was told that many who heard him reading from the Bible almost felt moved to leave the church immediately and go home to think about the message he had delivered in the reading. This commitment to quality and attention to detail was to become a hallmark of his work.

However on one occasion, when writing a letter of thanks to a lady after a preaching engagement, he made a mistake. At the end of the letter he added a Bible reference. He intended this to be Proverbs 10:22, but instead he wrote Proverbs 11:22. When she looked up the verse, rather than the one which says, 'The blessing of the LORD brings wealth, and he adds no trouble to it,' she read, 'As a jewel of gold in a swine's snout, so is a fair woman ... without discretion' (KJV). The bewildered lady wrote to ask for an explanation and John was able to put things right!

The next significant event for John and Joyce was the founding of the Guernsey branch of the National Young Life Campaign (NYLC), along with four other Christian friends. Here were six new Christians on a tiny island with no experience — but tons of enthusiasm and a passionate desire to share their faith with others.

Within two years they had stepped out in faith and organized the 'Guernsey for God' campaign. Amazingly, over sixty churches supported the campaign, providing leaders and forming a working committee with John as the General Secretary. Two NYLC speakers, Frank Farley and Ray Castro, led the fifteen-night campaign, which was held in the largest church on the island. Over a thousand prayer partners supported the event, from fifteen different countries. There was wide press coverage, and capacity crowds attended. Most importantly, many people became Christians and were then linked up to their nearest church. These were breathtaking results and made spiritual history on the island. God continued to bless the branch in a remarkable way and called over twenty of its members into full-time Christian service within the next seven years.

This event was also supported by the extremely gifted blind pianist Peter Jackson, and it was here that Peter met his future wife, Margaret. Peter and Margaret were to become very dear friends of John and Joyce over the coming years. Peter joined John on many other occasions, sharing the good news of the gospel by means of music and preaching.

3
A large place

By 1961 John was H. M. Deputy Sergeant to the Royal Court of Guernsey, which gave him a steady income and, above all else, job security. He and Joyce now had two sons, Christopher and Timothy, and were expecting their third child. John still found the time to commit to evangelistic work in all parts of Guernsey. Yet God had other plans for this little family.

The next time Frank Farley returned to Guernsey, he preached on the subject of Christian service and made a passionate call for Christians to commit to full-time evangelism. That night John had a sense that God was calling him into full-time service, but he also understood the enormous implications for his family. He returned home and told Joyce he had something he needed to discuss. Amazingly, with a prescience that was to become part of her, she already knew, and they talked and cried long into the night. This was such a huge step, and John had to be sure.

The next morning John turned to his daily Bible study notes and found a reference to a 'verse of the week'. Burdened with the decision that lay before him, he decided that if the verse said anything about his sense of call, he would do as it said. At the same time an inner voice said very clearly, 'You'll never be able to find the words to say.' This immediately filled him with negative thoughts about his limited experience and doubts about his capability to be a full-time preacher. He quickly opened his Bible to the 'verse of the week', which read, 'Now therefore go, and I will be with thy mouth, and teach thee what thou shalt say' (Exodus 4:12, KJV). The answer could not have been clearer.

The next day John applied to NYLC for a full-time post as an evangelist and was accepted. Suddenly he and Joyce were faced with the trauma of leaving their beloved island and moving to what seemed like an enormous foreign land — England. By this time there had been another addition to the family with the birth of their third son, Andrew. Finance was also a problem and they had no means of paying for the boat journey. A few days before they were due to leave, an envelope was pushed under their door. It contained the exact amount needed to pay for the journey. John had not asked anyone for help, but God knew his need and met it in a most remarkable way. His daily Bible reading also gave him great encouragement, especially Psalm 118:5, which said that the Lord had set him 'in a large place' (KJV). England seemed to him to be a very large place indeed, and he assumed that this would be the extent of his ministry.

Many tributes were made to John and Joyce as they left their church family in Guernsey. Joyce's work was fully acknowledged, not only as a committed witness to the Saviour, but also as a singer, secretary, committee member and magazine editor.

On 5 March 1962 the family moved from Guernsey to a tiny top-floor flat in Weston-Super-Mare, in the county of Somerset, and John became a full-time evangelist. Missing all the limelight was to become a feature of Joyce's life and one she was comfortable with. She was content to stay at home with her boys, quietly support-ing John in prayer and graciously enabling him to commit himself fully to the work that God had called him to do. He had no idea what lay ahead, or that his work would go far beyond anything he could have imagined. He heard of another young man starting out in the ministry who asked an older pastor for some advice. The pastor replied in one sentence: 'Lay the sinner low; lift the Saviour high.' John never forgot that advice and took it to heart, making it the overall aim of his preaching.

John's first engagement as a full-time evangelist was on 9 March 1962 at an NYLC house party held at Charterhouse, a Christian conference centre in Devon. Thereafter he toured round his 'parish' in the south-west of England, which consisted of the counties of Gloucester, Somerset, Dorset, Devon and Cornwall. There were no motorways, and the A38 became the 'longest lane in England' to him. His goal was to visit every NYLC branch on his patch with a view to spurring them into greater effort and re-energizing those which were on the point of closure. This was hard work, and not every branch survived. But many thrived, and at the end of his first year in full-time work he had taken 324 preaching engagements.

On one Good Friday he gave two boys a lift on his way through North Devon. As they chatted he asked whether they knew what day it was. Surprisingly they did and said it was the day Jesus died. When John asked them why he died, they replied that he died to save us from our sins. 'Has he done that for you?' asked John. There was a stunned silence and the question was never answered. One year later, John was preaching in the same area and after the service someone asked if he could speak to him. It was one of the boys he had picked up on the previous Good Friday.

The boy said he had been unable to forget the question John had asked and had been thinking about it for the past year. He knew that Jesus had not saved him from his sins and he said he was ready to put his trust in him. With John at his side, the boy placed his life in the hands of the one who died for him and finally met the risen Saviour.

On one occasion John returned home to be told by Joyce that he had received an invitation to speak at 'Albert Hall'. John assumed that this was the local Brethren assembly until he discovered that the invitation was to speak at the Royal Albert Hall in London at the annual London and Home Counties Festival of Male Voice Praise. This was John's first experience of speaking to a large audience and it was in a venue he had only previously seen on television. On 27 April 1963 John stood at the imposing podium and spoke to over 5,000 people, lifting the Saviour high. He read from Micah 6:8, which says: 'What does the LORD require of you? To act justly and to love mercy and to walk humbly with your God.'

In the next few years John focused on leading evangelistic campaigns in towns throughout the south-west, as well as a huge number of other single preaching engagements. His ministry was greatly blessed, and many people had a life-changing encounter with the Lord Jesus Christ. By now, a fourth son, Stephen, had been born and life on John's small salary was hard. Joyce knitted countless sweaters which were carefully mended and handed down their growing line of sons, the youngest son becoming accustomed to wearing clothes that had previously been worn by all his brothers. She proved herself to be a very efficient manager of slender resources and shared John's conviction about priorities. Yet, whatever their financial constraints, Joyce had a heart full of compassion for those in need. When sugar was in short supply, she gave a large bag to her pastor, telling him his needs were greater than hers. She always helped in whatever way she could and was a living expression of obedience to Jesus' command: 'Freely you have received, freely give' (Matthew 10:8).

On one occasion their own needs were met in an amazing way. They lived in a very cold house, and this always reminded John of an American who visited the UK in winter. He told friends he had stayed in an unusual house with five refrigerators — 'They called them bedrooms!' John felt he could identify with that. Their home had a coal fire in one room as the single source of heat. One morning Joyce reminded John that they had almost run out of coal. John rang the coalman and arranged an immediate delivery. It was only as the last sack was being emptied into their backyard that John realized he had no money to pay the bill. At that moment the postman arrived and handed John an envelope. It contained the exact amount of cash needed to pay the coalman. On reflection, John was amazed at God's detailed provision. Someone had been moved to send money to the family. They had decided on exactly the right amount to cover the cost of the coal. They had posted the letter at exactly the right moment so that it was delivered that morning, and the postman had somehow timed his delivery to perfection. None of that had anything to do with John, but it had everything to do with the Saviour.

On one of his evening preaching engagements John surprised his audience by telling them that he had enough money to last for the rest of his life. Then he added, 'And I have it all with me in my pocket.' He went on to say that as it was 9 p.m. and the shops were all closed, and because Jesus might come back at any moment, as far as he knew he had enough money to last for the rest of his life. This absolute trust in God's provision underpinned John and Joyce's married life and his ministry.

By 1964 John's friend Frank Farley had joined the Movement for World Evangelization (MWE). He invited John to attend their annual Christian Holiday Crusade at Butlin's Holiday Camp in Filey, North Yorkshire. John attended as an observer but suddenly found himself speaking to 1,000 teenagers at their nightly 'Teen Time' event. As a result of this visit he was told that he would be welcome to join MWE as one of their evangelists. However, at that time he was heavily involved in preparing for 'Crusade 65', a three-week evangelistic outreach across the whole of the island of Jersey. It was to be a remarkable campaign, led by John and his fellow evangelist Doug Barnett and backed by a team of seventy helpers. Over 15,000 people attended many different events in a wide range of venues, including youth clubs, nightclubs and dance halls. One of these events marked John's 1,000th engagement as a full-time evangelist. The campaign also produced a surprising outcome when John was invited by Channel Television to make his first TV appearance. On Palm Sunday, 11 April 1964, John took over the thirty-minute 'God slot' and presented the gospel to the island of Jersey. Many people came to faith in Jesus Christ as a result of the campaign, and the event had a lasting effect on the island. It was to mark a change of direction for John, who felt that God was calling him to follow a different path. In the following year he accepted the invitation to join MWE.

4
Openings and opportunities

As an MWE evangelist John was soon involved in another major event, 'Crusade 66', which covered the whole of North Devon. Over 20,000 people heard the gospel, which was preached at hundreds of meetings across 250 square miles of the county. During this crusade his fifth son, Michael, was born and John was presented with a bar of the then popular Fry's 'Five Boys' chocolate!

In 1966 John wrote his first book. He understood the importance of Bible reading to new Christians, to help them learn more about God and to discover his purpose for their lives. It was common practice at that time to give new Christians a copy of the Gospel of John, but he felt that something else was needed. *Read Mark Learn* divided the Gospel of Mark into forty-five daily readings, taking the reader through Mark's record of the earthly life of Jesus. John was not to know that in later years God would use his writing to become a worldwide ministry.

In that same year John visited Northern Ireland for the first time. While Christianity was flourishing, the Province was about to enter the 'Troubles', a thirty-year period of conflict between the mainly Protestant Unionists and the mainly Roman Catholic Nationalists. John's engagements included a Christian Workers' Union rally in Co. Antrim and an opportunity to share the gospel with 200 inmates of Crumlin Road Prison in Belfast. This was the beginning of a long-lasting relationship with the troubled Province. It was the first of many visits and the start of some very valuable friendships.

On 1 January 1967, John visited Greece for the first time, supporting pastors with the provision of Bible study materials and speaking in Katerini, Berea, Sevasti and Thessalonica. His planned preaching schedule was abandoned when he began to feel extremely unwell and a doctor diagnosed 'neurosis of the heart'. He was forced to rest for the remainder of his stay — something he does not do easily!

At this time John had a keen interest in the Slavic Gospel Association. In April 1967 he joined the secretary of the organization and one of the council members on a two-week tour preaching in mission centres in France, Germany, Austria and Yugoslavia.

In the same year MWE took over the responsibility for the daily Christian ministry at the Highlands Hotel on the island of Jersey. John was delighted to speak at the hotel on 9 July — despite the fact that to a Guernsey man Jersey is the 'inferior' island! John often tells people that the best thing about Jersey is that on a clear day you can see Guernsey! Six years earlier, John had preached in St Matthew's Church, Jersey, and had succeeded in irritating Ron Brint, the youth leader there, intensely. However, God was working on Ron's heart in the same way he had previously worked on the young John Blanchard's heart when he was a religious youth leader. At the end of the week Ron became a Christian and a year later he resigned his post as a police detective to become manager of the Highlands Hotel. John's connection with the hotel was to continue for the next twenty years and provided a very rare holiday opportunity for the Blanchard family.

As he travelled more widely, John's absence presented an enormous challenge to Joyce, which she faced with remarkable patience and grace. She became very close to her five sons and was delighted when John's annual speaking engagement at the hotel allowed him to take his family along free of charge. By this time John was utterly convinced that 'a boy is a skin stretched over an appetite', and he greatly appreciated having free meals for his 'five rascals' and sharing two precious weeks together with Joyce.

This was followed by hundreds of engagements in the next few years, including campaigns in England and house parties in Norway and Switzerland. He also hosted a tour of the Holy Land during the celebrations of the twentieth anniversary of the creation of the State of Israel and preached in Jerusalem and Nazareth.

The door to Eastern Europe opened unexpectedly and, although this was not John's vision or idea, it was one of those moments of inexplicable guidance. It led to him and two other MWE colleagues making eighty visits during which many people found faith in Jesus Christ, churches were encouraged and Christians strengthened. Taking the good news of the gospel behind the 'Iron Curtain' became a feature of John's ministry and something that came to be very close to his heart.

In 1968 he paid his first visit to Brno Baptist Church in what was then Czechoslovakia. The day started with a packed prayer meeting at 9 a.m. There had already been four sermons before John started to preach and later in the day he was asked to preach again, such was the hunger for God's Word. This was an unforgettable introduction to Christianity behind the Iron Curtain and only served to increase John's desire to become further involved in work in that country. He returned in April 1968 and asked fellow-evangelist Peter Anderson to go with him.

Then, on 28 January 1970, they set out once again for Czechoslovakia with MWE colleague and singer Eric Clarke. The three of them drove cautiously towards Checkpoint Charlie, the best-known crossing point in the Berlin Wall. An armed guard examined their personal papers and then asked for the documents relating to the car. However, the registration book was in the name of the Movement for World Evangelization, which would surely prevent them from entering Communist Eastern Europe. With his mind racing, John left the registration book in the car and handed the guard a wad of impressive-looking literature issued by Volkswagen. Amazingly, the man glanced at this and waved them into Eastern Germany.

The three men left Berlin as fast as they could and headed for Warsaw, just over 300 miles to the east. Heavy snow slowed them down, but when they reached the Polish border they faced another crisis. At the remote border post their personal papers were accepted, but then they were told to submit the entire contents of the car for examination. This was a problem because of one particular item. Another Christian organization had asked them to deliver 'some tapes' to a church in Warsaw. Geography was not John's strongest point and he had agreed to this, assuming it would not be much of a diversion. He was wrong by several hundred miles. He had made another assumption that the tapes would be a few small cassettes, which could easily be hidden away. Instead they had a large box of fifty reel-to-reel audio tapes with nowhere to hide them. 'What are these?' asked the guard. 'A gift from the church in England to the church in Poland,' replied John carefully. 'This is too much', the guard replied, before disappearing into another room. Moments later he returned and in perfect English ordered, 'Get this out of here before the boss gets back.' Needless to say, that order was obeyed extremely quickly and soon they were safely in Warsaw, where they checked into a nondescript and extremely cold hotel.

On the following morning they began to search for Warsaw's United Evangelical Church. Afraid of speaking to someone who might be hostile to Christianity, they dared not ask directions, but after less than an hour of criss-crossing the city they found what they were looking for. The building was similar to the many surrounding piles of dreary East European architecture, but something convinced them that they had found the right place. It was the symbol of a cross — a simple and courageous witness to Jesus Christ in a hostile place. The tapes were received with enormous gratitude and after preaching there the men continued to Krakow, where they were given an emotional welcome as the first Christians from the West to visit the church since the Iron Curtain had come down.

There were many far-reaching results of these visits. Several Czech pastors visited the MWE week at Filey and over the next few years MWE team members took pastors on speaking tours around the UK, providing them with clothing and meeting other practical needs.

In 1969 John was nominated by MWE to preach in the United States of America and he crossed the Atlantic for the first time. He visited Michigan, Washington State and Idaho, little knowing that he would make that journey many, many times in the future and preach at over 400 Bible Conferences across the USA.

No one who has ever met John would be left in any doubt about his devotion to the game of golf. Surprisingly, he had never played the game until 1971, when he was almost forty years old. MWE's President, Lindsay Glegg, advised him to take up the game as a means of recreation. When John said he was too busy Lindsay replied, 'My boy' (every man was 'My boy' to him), 'as I told Billy Graham, Alan Redpath, Stephen Olford and others, you must take up golf. It will add years to your life.'

As always, finance was an issue and John could not afford golf clubs or the fees to join a club. A secondhand set of golf clubs was provided by another MWE member and soon a lone figure could be seen in the evenings hitting golf balls along the beach at Weston-Super-Mare. John was hooked, and so began an ongoing love for the game, which he still plays enthusiastically today, continually adding more silverware to his overcrowded trophy cabinet. He is a meticulous record-keeper and has details of every golf game he has ever played, as many an unsuspecting host has discovered when John is a guest in their home!

The trophy that gave him the greatest delight was the one presented to the Free Church Ministers' Golf Society by Samuel Ryder in 1902. Knowing the international status, in the golfing world, of the now famous Ryder Cup, the society proudly refers to their trophy as 'the first Ryder Cup'. John won this on five occasions between 1994 and 2007. In 1978 he was invited to speak at the annual Christian Golfers' Conference, held that year in Co. Donegal, in the Republic of Ireland. This was the beginning of yet more valued friendships and tenacious pot-hunting! He has been the speaker on seven occasions since then and was captain of the conference in 1990.

Needless to say, John has taken every opportunity to combine golf with his ministry and has spoken at many golf days on both sides of the Atlantic. Many of these events enable him to speak to players with no interest in Christianity and to give them gospel literature. One such event in California resulted in a well-known public official becoming a Christian. The man later sent John a gold-plated putter inscribed with his name and a text from the book of Hebrews: 'Jesus Christ, the same yesterday, and today and for ever' (Hebrews 13:8, KJV). Golf has become a major fitness factor in John's life and a delightful way of releasing the pressures involved in his heavy schedule of writing, preaching and travelling.

In 1971 John wrote his second book. It was called *Right with God* and was his response to the need for a straightforward presentation of the gospel to help anyone searching for a personal faith in God. It was published in September of that year and to date almost 400,000 copies have been sold. It has been translated into thirteen languages and also produced in Braille by the Torch Trust for the Blind. As with all his books, John's desire was that it should be used to bring many people to know Jesus personally.

Over the years John has received encouraging feedback relating to this book, which has confirmed his purpose in writing it. One man lent his copy to ten friends in turn, and nine of them came to know Jesus Christ as their Saviour. John heard that five members of the same family had each become a Christian after reading the book. An Indian man who was descended from a long line of idol-worshippers found faith in the true God while reading the book. A touching story came from a lady in South Africa who received the Afrikaans version of it. She wanted to give a copy to a friend but could not afford it. She did the only thing possible — she painstakingly wrote it out word for word and sent it to her friend. After reading it the friend came to know the Saviour. In particular John appreciated the story of a car thief who found a copy in a car he had stolen, read it, gave his life to Christ on the spot and promptly returned the car to its rightful owner! John takes no credit for these things but is very thankful that God continues to use *Right with God* in this wonderful way.

Later that year the family moved to Croydon and John was appointed MWE's first Director of Evangelism. In 1972 he returned once more to the island of Jersey for 'Crusade 72'. Peter Anderson and Derek Cleave joined him in leading a team to set up a wide range of events across the island. Meetings were held in schools, colleges, hospitals and prisons. There were Rotary Club and police lunches and an open-air meeting in the Howard Davis Park in St Helier. Channel Television ran a series of epilogues and the island saw the opening of its first Christian bookshop. Many of the islanders who joined the team had become Christians during the previous crusade, in 1965, and were able to testify to the continuing reality of their faith in God.

It was at this time that Joyce started to slip slowly into a period of depression. Despite medical attention, she suffered many months of seeming darkness and shed many tears. John eventually realized that his days as a travelling evangelist might well be numbered. He went to speak at the 'Keswick in Greece' Convention in Leptokaria in August 1974 and decided that if there was no change in Joyce's condition on his return, this would be his last tour. From his window in Leptokaria he could see a group of Greek women who met every morning to pray. When he spoke to them, one of them told him that Joyce would be better when he returned home. 'But you don't know just how sick she is,' replied John quietly.

When he arrived at Heathrow Airport on his return to England, he rang home. The phone was answered by an upbeat voice he did not immediately recognize. It was Joyce. She told him how two people had, independently of one another, sent her letters while John was away, both saying the same thing — that God is under no obligation to explain anything he sends or allows in our lives. That did not instantly cure her, but she had a sudden deep conviction that she was safe in God's hands even if he did not explain her circumstances. That was the turning point, and when John returned home she was waiting to share this truth with him. This was yet more evidence of God's great goodness to them and Joyce was enabled to continue in her steadfast support for John's widening ministry.

In 1975 John preached at the famous Westminster Chapel in London at the Diamond Jubilee service of the Girl Crusaders' Union. He was invited to return in early 1976, and on this occasion was asked by Sir Fred Catherwood and the deacons if he would be willing to allow his name to go forward as the prospective minister of the church. Totally floored, John simply said, 'You're crazy!' He would have to follow in the footsteps of the legendary Dr Martin Lloyd-Jones, who had been its powerful and devout minister for thirty years. All John's doubts about his suitability were put aside by the deacons and finally he allowed his name to go forward. He preached at the chapel on 4 July and was overwhelmed by the response of members who desperately wanted him to be their minister. Added to this was the conviction of Dr Lloyd-Jones himself that John was the man for the job.

Despite this John still had doubts which left him in great turmoil. This would be a very different role and one that would lead him in a totally new direction. Accepting this job would limit his ministry to one place of worship. In his heart he still believed that he was best suited to being on the road and travelling widely as an evangelist. On 13 September, after much prayer, serious consideration and many sleepless nights, John finally declined the invitation. Both John and Joyce felt that he had made the right decision, although Joyce would have faithfully stood by him had he accepted the post.

Some time later Dr R. T. Kendall was appointed as minister at Westminster Chapel. He sent one of his books to John inscribed with the following: 'For John Blanchard, the man who might have been, from the man who was.' Events since then have shown that John's decision was the right one, as today he still travels extensively preaching the gospel and defending the Christian faith.

Another trip to America saw him in Dalhart, Texas, in October 1976. He preached at two morning services, dashed out during the last hymn and was taken to a grass landing strip for a daunting take-off in a two-seater 'crop-duster' bound for Amarillo. From there he caught a scheduled flight to Dallas; then there was another flight and a final dash from the airport to get him to his evening preaching engagement. He is a great travelling man and still enjoys the challenge of tight schedules, airport dashes and impossible destinations.

An event which took place in Torquay in 1977 was to prompt John to write another book many years later. He was invited to speak at a house meeting one evening, but only four people arrived, three of whom were Christians. With only one, a successful businessman, needing to hear the good news of the gospel, John felt strangely unsure what to say. This man was clearly not impressed when John began to read a 2,000-year-old sermon from the Bible, first delivered by Jesus himself and written down by Matthew in chapters 5 – 7 of his Gospel. By the time John came to the end of the reading, however, the man was on the edge of his seat, not wanting to miss a single word. That evening had a lasting effect on both the businessman and the preacher and was a testimony to the power of the Bible as the 'living and enduring word of God' (1 Peter 1:23).

It was some years later that John decided to write a commentary on the first twelve verses of Matthew chapter 5, known as the Beatitudes. Eventually, after he had discussed this with two pastor friends, in 1996 three books were published: *The Beatitudes for Today* by John Blanchard, *The Ten Commandments for Today* by Brian Edwards and *The Lord's Prayer for Today* by Derek Prime.

The next three years included several preaching engagements in the United States. In April 1978 he spoke at America's 'Keswick in Whiting', New Jersey, and then backtracked to Southcliffe Baptist Church, Fort Worth, to preach to large crowds in the church and to 2,000 faculty members and students at Southwestern

Baptist Theological Seminary. He returned in 1980 to take the Bible studies at the Texas Baptist Evangelism Conference, speaking to audiences of around 8,000, many of whom were pastors and staff members. Three additional weeks in America included thirteen services at the 'Moody Keswick' Bible Conference in St Petersburg, Florida.

5
And then there were three

In early 1980, John, along with two other MWE evangelists, Peter Anderson and Derek Cleave, felt led by God to leave MWE and link their work more closely together. On 1 April of that same year Christian Ministries (CM) was brought into being. A national newspaper called it the 'ABC of evangelism', from the initials of the three surnames (Anderson, Blanchard and Cleave). The team worked both independently and together, enjoying an extremely close and united relationship based on complete trust in God and in each other.

An early sign of God's blessing on this project was a gift of £12,000, which covered the cost of the cars needed to continue their itinerant ministries. Mervyn and Helen Snow became CM's honorary administrators and carried out this task for over twenty years with great efficiency and integrity. Over the same period of time John was assisted in the typing of his books and letters by Joy Harling, and this was a great practical help to him.

In June 1980 John was invited to speak at a series of services at Barcombe Baptist Church, East Sussex. He felt privileged to share the ministry with Dr Martyn Lloyd-Jones, especially as this included the final sermon that Lloyd-Jones was to preach: he died on 1 March 1981.

During the 1980s John continued to visit Eastern Europe. At the same time his ministry in the USA grew ever wider and he completed over forty preaching tours, speaking at nearly 1,000 services. The venues varied from the tiny town of Cut and Shoot in Texas, with a population of only a few hundred, to Washington DC, the capital of the USA. John carefully records his travels, and on one of these tours he noted the fact that he had completed his first million miles as an evangelist.

While giving his testimony in Los Angeles, John recounted how he had become a Christian after listening to the preaching of Paul Cantelon in 1954 on the island of Guernsey. He said he would love to meet Paul to tell him what happened on that October night all those years ago. At the end of the service a lady said she knew Paul and gave his address to John. On his return to England John wrote a letter of thanks to Paul for what, with God's gracious enabling, he had done on that night. Paul received the letter when he was going through a particularly tough time and he was greatly uplifted by the contents. He sent an immediate and warm response saying that he had left Guernsey feeling that the campaign had been a failure, and so he was overjoyed by John's news. He invited John to preach at a Bible conference at his church, Calvary Temple, Bellingham, in Washington. John gladly accepted the invitation and thus met Paul for the first time — on the twenty-sixth anniversary of the day when he became a Christian.

While John was at Bellingham, his daily reading covered the subject of the apostle Paul's conversion and baptism. He had thought for some time about being baptized, but had never taken that step. Suddenly he knew that he had to do so, and he asked Paul if he could be baptized at his church. That night John gave his testimony to a hushed congregation, many of whom were in tears, including Paul himself, as they heard how, in the goodness of God, their pastor had been used to touch a young man's life in such a miraculous way. Paul then baptized John, the two men no longer strangers, but dear friends and brothers in Christ.

As John was leaving the church a lady asked him whether he planned to share the experience with his wife in England. John was at the beginning of a three-week trip and could only afford to ring Joyce at the end of each week. The lady worked for the local telephone company and she arranged for John to make a free call. Joyce was surprised to receive a phone call so early in an overseas trip, but when John said he wanted to share the wonderful church service with her she said, 'You were baptized.' 'How did you know?' asked John. He could sense the smile on her face. 'I just knew,' she said in her lovely way, which was part of their close-ness to each other and to the Lord.

A year later Joyce was struggling with another period of depression. Travelling to their home church was difficult for her during John's absences and so they felt it was the right time to move from Croydon. As always, finance was an issue, but once again God's hand was on them. Unexpected help was received and in October 1981 the family moved to the village of Banstead in Surrey, where John still lives today. During their time at their previous house, a nameplate with the name 'Sarnia' (which is the old Roman name for Guernsey) had been given to them by MWE colleagues as a lovely reminder of their island roots. This very important item travelled with the family to Banstead and is still in use there today.

22 August 1982 was the occasion of their Silver Wedding, and Joyce was able to join John on a preaching tour. Their special milestone was celebrated in Carlsbad, California, but only after he had preached three times on that day!

That year Evangelical Press (EP) became John's publishers and released his devotional commentary on the epistle of James. *Truth for Life* took a very honest and practical look at the epistle, showing its dynamic relevance to all Christians down the ages as they battle to overcome the world, the flesh and the devil. The book was revised and reprinted in 2004. James has always been one of John's favourite books and over the years he has spent thousands of hours 'tunnelling into the text' to discover its meaning and to apply it to the everyday realities of living in the modern world. In his book he described the epistle as practical, pastoral and penetrating. In the foreword to *Truth for Life* Sir Fred Catherwood wrote, 'Our generation of Christians needs the epistle of James as few generations before have needed it ... we need to be reminded again that faith without works is dead.'

For several years the three CM evangelists had been concerned about the increase in 'entertainment evangelism', and in 1983 Derek and Peter helped John to write a book called *Pop Goes the Gospel* which looked at current approaches to evangelism, and rock music in particular. The book examined the history of rock and pop music. It asked readers to base their approach to outreach, and to every area of their lives, on consistent biblical principles. At the annual Christian Booksellers' Convention, this publication was nominated as one of the most significant books of the year. As a result John was asked to preach on the subject on many occasions. One of these was at the 1984 Evangelical Movement of Wales Conference in Aberystwyth. He preached at an evening meeting and was then asked to speak again to a group of young people. So many came that the venue had to be changed and the interaction between speaker and listeners, which John always encouraged, continued until midnight.

Although the book was welcomed in some circles, it was certainly not popular in others, especially among those involved in the Christian music business. In 2006 John co-wrote *Can we Rock the Gospel?* with Dan Lucarini, an American musician, songwriter and worship leader. Once again the book was loved by some and hated by others. That year both men received thousands of letters, emails and phone calls in an extraordinary response to the publication. They were severely criticized by many and, while this was expected, it was a less than pleasant experience at times. Yet they were also encouraged by the number of readers who commended the book and thanked them for addressing this

particular issue. Many readers admitted that the
content of the book had led them to think again about
the subject and to adopt a more biblical approach to
worship and outreach.

John's next publication after *Pop Goes the Gospel* was
written as a result of his concern about the lack of a
really good evangelistic booklet. He took his idea to EP
in the vain hope that a high-quality booklet illustrated
with superb colour pictures could be produced
cheaply. He was quickly brought down to earth with a
realistic quote of the likely cost, which was far higher
than he had anticipated. Not to be outdone, he set
about raising the money. As a result *Ultimate Questions*
was published on 5 March 1987, which coincided with
the twenty-fifth anniversary of John's first day in full-
time ministry. The first print run was set at an ambi-
tious 100,000, but was sold out before it reached the
publisher's warehouse. Churches ordered hundreds,
and even thousands, of the booklet at a time. Soon there
was a demand for foreign translations. One order of
400,000 copies was sent to Russia to be used as part of a
three-week project, during which 45,000 people responded to gospel articles published in a secular
newspaper.

The booklet included the offer of a free copy of *Read
Mark Learn*, and the publishers were almost swamped
with requests. Tricia Rubens (the wife of the General

Manager of EP at the time, John Rubens) offered to
send these out on a voluntary basis. As she did so,
people came back with more questions and requests for
further books to help with Bible study. This was just the
start of the booklet's impact, and no one could have
foreseen how widely it would be used in the coming
years.

In 1985 the CM Board started fund-raising for missionary work in India. Money was raised for church buildings, a Bible School and an orphanage for 300 children.
John and the two other CM evangelists made many
visits to the southern state of Andhra Pradesh in
subsequent years and continued to send funds for
evangelists' salaries, medical supplies, food for or-
phans, a jeep, mopeds and bicycles. All three evangelists delivered Bible teaching to pastors and evangelists
and also preached at many services in large cities, such
as Madras and Hyderabad, as well as in many smaller
village locations.

While John will always be a Guernsey man at heart, he
still has a lasting affection for the Isle of Islay, his home
as an evacuee during the war years. He always wanted
to return there and share the gospel with the islanders,
and he did this twice in the 1980s. He spoke in a community centre in Port Ellen and at Islay Hospital. He
also returned to the school where he had been a pupil

and met a lady who remembered teaching him forty years earlier.

John arranged for a copy of *Ultimate Questions* to be given to every household on the island, and the Baptist pastor Jon Magee took on the task of delivering them. One of his visits was to the island's largest and most imposing residence, Islay House. Jon explained to the owner that the booklet had been written by a wartime evacuee and that the author would be returning to the island to speak at several meetings. The man immediately offered to host one of the meetings, and on 28 October 1987 around eighty people attended an outreach buffet.

Some time after this the Christian Television Association made a film of John's testimony and ministry entitled *Journey into Life*, and this was shown at several venues on the island. John also wrote an evangelistic article for the island's newspaper, *Ileach*, and he was told of several people finding faith in Christ as a result.

In 1988 John made his first visit to South Africa. This lasted for three weeks, during which he travelled across the whole country and spoke at over eighty events. As if this wasn't enough, another event was added when a group of Christians in KwaZulu-Natal discovered that he had a free day. As a result he preached to a packed school hall in Pietermaritzburg. In Cape Town he preached at several services in St

James Church, Kenilworth. He was not to know that seven years later this church would be attacked by terrorists who killed eleven worshippers and wounded fifty-eight others. He was also given media opportunities and made several radio broadcasts. He had a television interview with Frank Retief, Rector of St James, who later became Presiding Bishop of the Church of England in South Africa.

John has always acknowledged the hand of God in many of the delightful coincidences he has experienced. On one occasion he was preaching in South Wales and suddenly, for no apparent reason, he found himself sharing with his hearers a recent experience in Czechoslovakia. At the end of the evening a man approached him and said that he had heard John speak before — at his home church in Czechoslovakia. His name was Robert Poloha, and he had been the pastor there but had been forced to escape to the West. He had an enormous burden for his country, but had no way of returning home. John, by another delightful 'coincidence', had arranged to meet with the head of Trans World Radio on the following day to discuss gospel broadcasts to Czechoslovakia. This resulted in an amazing ministry for Robert and he made over twenty broadcasts a week to the people of his homeland for the next twenty years. He received an enormous response, including countless letters from people who were challenged, strengthened and, most importantly, brought to faith in the Lord Jesus Christ as a result of the broadcasts.

John marked the tenth anniversary of CM by a round-the-world tour. This began with three days' ministry to the staff of the Overseas Missionary Fellowship in Hang Nam, Thailand. The next stop was Australia, where he spent eighteen days in Tamworth, Armidale, Newcastle, Sydney, Albury, Melbourne, Ballarat, Kerang and Tasmania. Events included church services, five pastors' conferences, youth rallies and lectures in theological colleges.

The next port of call was New Zealand, where he spoke at seven events, six of them at a Reformed Baptist Conference in Auckland. He then crossed the International Date Line to speak in Hawaii, and this resulted in an intriguing situation. He preached on Sunday evening in Auckland and then arrived in Hawaii *on the morning of the same day* to speak at the morning service in University Avenue Baptist Church, Honolulu!

He completed several days of ministry in Hawaii before flying to California, where he spoke over the Easter weekend in Santa Barbara. He also spoke at Westmont College and the University of California. He completed eight more days of ministry in Doyline, Louisiana and Marietta, Georgia, before flying home to complete his 30,000 mile tour.

Soon after his return his stepmother, who still lived on Guernsey, had major surgery. John and Joyce flew to the island to be with her, but while they were there they received news that their home had been burgled. John flew back to oversee the situation and secure the premises. He then returned to Guernsey just in time for both him and Joyce to be with his stepmother when she died. Her last words were: 'I love Jesus and I love you.'

Towards the end of 1990 John completed a further seven-week tour of the United States and then, in late 1991, he started another sixty-day visit which took him to Georgia, Tennessee, South Carolina, Mississippi, Alabama, Louisiana and Florida. Events included a three-day Bible conference at the historic First Presbyterian Church, Augusta, Georgia, and nine engagements in the Independent Presbyterian Church in Savannah. He then preached at First Presbyterian Church, Jackson, Mississippi, and he and Joyce were to visit this church many times in the future, making some very close friendships. On one of these visits, in 1993, his five-hour School of Personal Evangelism was filmed and this was subsequently issued in both US and European format.

In early 1991 John spoke at the Carey Ministers Conference at the Hayes Conference Centre, Swanwick, in the UK. He shared the ministry with the American Professor Don Carson. John's subject was 'The impact and thrust of preaching'. A press report of this event said:

> All his preaching and writings speak of the bene-
> fits of labour. No one else has developed so acute
> a homiletical mind. But it is not in Blanchard's
> acknowledged gift of communication that his
> strength lies. It is in his theology and the fresh-
> ness with which he applies it to the conscience
> and affections of his hearers.

John is the first to acknowledge Almighty God as the giver of his gifts and skills. He has often regretted his lack of tertiary education but, after becoming a Christian at the age of twenty-two, he studied the Bible with an ever-increasing passion. He is an avid reader and over the years has read widely. He is blessed with a razor-sharp intellect and is able to research and then communicate difficult subjects with clarity and logic. This has enabled him to have a clear and uncompromising commitment to the doctrines of the Reformers and the Puritans. His ministry is based on the solid foundation of salvation through faith alone, by grace alone, through Scripture alone. John believes totally in the absolute sovereignty of God and in the election of all who will be saved. He was once asked how he reconciled election and evangelism. He replied, 'Election is a doctrine I am called to believe, and evangelism is a command I am called to obey. So I believe the first and obey the second.'

1992 was to be another hectic year. John was invited to Haven Holiday Camp, Caister-on-Sea, for the annual Fellowship of Independent Evangelical Churches (FIEC) conference. He had previously spoken at this event in 1982 when it was held in Westminster Chapel, London. This time he gave three Bible studies on the Minor Prophets, not knowing that twenty years later he would write a book based on the importance of their messages.

Later that year he flew to Brazil, where he gave eight hour-long messages on the subject of 'Evangelism in the light of God's Word' at the FIEL Conference for pastors and church leaders in Aguas de Lindoia.

He also took six sessions at a pastors' conference in Magaliesburg, Gauteng, South Africa, which was to lead to invitations to many bigger conferences in the future. One pastor had travelled from Namibia with the intention of resigning from the ministry, but by the end of the conference God had graciously used John's ministry to change his mind and renew his commitment. On that visit John also spoke to teens and twenties at a conference in the Drakensberg Mountains, KwaZulu-Natal.

Writing was now playing a much bigger part in John's ministry and one particular subject was constantly on his mind. On a trip to Australia he asked the manager of a large Christian bookshop how many books he had on the subject of hell. His answer was 'None'. The reply did not surprise John, but it troubled him. Some time later he asked a minister how many books he had on that subject in his extensive personal library. The man replied that he had one, but could not find it. John's concern was that a fundamental biblical doctrine was being neglected, yet it was a vital part of the Christian message and needed to be addressed. The Bible's message is clear that if you do not repent and turn to Jesus Christ as your Lord while here on earth you will thereafter be in the presence of a holy God for ever — a just God who will then show you no mercy, no love and no forgiveness. People are not separated from God for ever when they die, wrote John. They are separated from his love, his grace, his mercy and his patience, but not from his presence. Hell is the presence of a God who is no longer willing to forgive, to love and to have mercy on those who are there. Nothing in the world can take us where God is not, either in this world or in the world to come. One of John's friends is a retired captain with American Airlines who flew inter-continental flights and spent most of his working life 30,000 feet above the planet. When asked for his fa-vourite verse in the Bible he quoted Psalm 139:7:

Where can I go from your Spirit?
Where can I flee from your presence?
If I go up to the heavens, you are there;
if I make my bed in the depths [literally, 'hell'],
     you are there.

Not even those who spend eternity in hell will have escaped the presence of God — because God is there.

The Bible also says the ungodly 'will be tormented ... in the presence of ... the Lamb' (Revelation 14:10). This is a terrifying truth for those who hate God or who do not believe he exists. The Bible tells us that one day 'every tongue [will] confess that Jesus Christ is Lord' (Philippians 2:11) and, as John says, 'this will be the loudest sound in hell'.

Faced with the urgency of the message, John began to write. The project meant long hours in his study and for Joyce it meant many weeks when he was virtually incommunicado. Yet the need to write about this difficult theme drove him on. 'The plight of the lost is so terrible, the power of sin so great and the horror of hell so fearful,' he wrote, 'how can I possibly do nothing to warn people of their danger and to point them to the Saviour?' In 1993 *Whatever Happened to Hell?* was published and it soon became a bestseller. It was translated into Braille and became available from the National Library for the Blind.

The following year proved to be just as busy, with a constant stream of invitations from all over the world. On a visit to Florida John was seen walking with a limp. During a game of golf in England he had gallantly offered to rescue his partner's ball from a ditch and had broken his leg in the attempt. Needless to say, this did not affect his ability to travel or to talk! He spoke at Pensacola Theological Institute, sharing the ministry with James Montgomery Boice, minister of Tenth Presbyterian Church, Philadelphia, and Michael Scott Horton, the then President of Christians United for Reformation. The institute's host said this had been the finest such event for a long time, with the highest book sales on record, which was a valuable extension of the ministry.

Most people remember where they were when the news broke of the tragic death of Diana, Princess of Wales on 31 August 1997. John was getting ready to preach in the Free Church of Scotland in Dornoch. He abandoned his planned sermon and preached on what happens after death. He reminded the congregation that death was a certainty and God's judgement a reality. He then shared the good news of the gospel of Jesus Christ, which is the answer to man's greatest need.

In the same year a retired merchant navy captain working as an evangelist in Antwerp decided to place a copy of *Ultimate Questions* in every home in Holland. He raised the necessary funds and during October nearly six million copies were delivered by mail and 155,000 delivered by hand. This had a far-reaching effect, with thousands of people writing to say they had found faith in Jesus Christ and asking for a free copy of *Read Mark Learn*.

Later that year John made a return visit to lecture at the Genesis Project, which had been launched in 1992 at Hook Evangelical Church in Surbiton, Surrey. He was extremely supportive of the project and found it to be one of the most encouraging enterprises he had ever seen in a local church. Since its inception, several hundred people had taken a two-year course covering church history, biblical theology, Christian leadership and many current contentious issues.

6
The big book

As the 1990s drew to a close, John felt deeply concerned about the rising tide of atheism, agnosticism and scepticism in the United Kingdom. He felt increasingly drawn to doing something about this growing problem and in 1997, supported by a group of praying friends, he started to write a 'small' book of about 150 pages to counteract it. But the more he researched, the more the book grew. It eventually came to be over 650 pages long, with a quarter of a million words and over 2,300 references from about 900 sources. Amazingly, John had not yet invested in a computer and the whole book was drafted by hand. This meant that Joy Harling had the enormous task of deciphering John's 'dreadful scrawl', and did so willingly and cheerfully. The typed manuscript was sent to his publishers, EP, in 1999.

Writing the book gave John a very different focus and he became convinced that his ministry was to take a completely new direction. Publication was due in March 2000 and he had already started to make plans to launch the book and its message in every county in the British Isles. He was over retirement age by now but was absolutely convinced that the Lord was calling him to devote his ministry to apologetics — challenging atheism and equipping Christians to do the same. This included countering the scientific, philosophical and religious objectives to 'the faith that was once for all entrusted to the saints' (Jude 3) and showing that the only true God has revealed himself in the Bible, in creation, in the human conscience and in the Lord Jesus Christ.

This was to place him at the front end of the battle to defend Christianity. It was to be his toughest challenge and would lead to great opposition and personal attack. Despite being given a serious health warning by his doctor, that he needed to 'slow down', the words of 1 Peter 3:15, 'Always be prepared to give an answer to everyone who asks you to give the reason for the hope that you have,' spurred him on to greater effort.

With a great sense of urgency and growing excitement, many ideas and objectives were already teeming in his head. Then John began to wonder how he could achieve them all while working on his own. He did not realize that God was to bring a complete stranger into his life to support him in this new and extremely challenging phase of his ministry. The man was Howard Williams and, at the time, their meeting in November 1999 seemed to be a coincidence. The common denominator was golf, and both had been invited by a pastor friend to stay at his apartment in Malaga for a week's golf. One day their host was laid low with food poisoning and so the two men went out for a meal together. In conversation Howard discovered something of John's aims and the launch plans for his book. He felt the urgency of John's mission and knew immediately that he wanted to support him in any way he could. This proved to be the start of a very close friendship and an ongoing involvement in John's apologetics ministry.

As 1999 drew to a close, there was intense interest in the arrival of the new millennium. The time and money spent in planning the celebrations to mark this event were beyond calculation. What was it all about, and why was there so much interest in this day? John wrote a book called *Why Y2K?*, which explained that the millennium was all about Jesus of Nazareth, whose birth divided history into two. John answered vital questions: 'Who was this man? Was he God? And why does it matter?' A special Guernsey edition was produced and, with the help of the Guernsey Evangelical

Fellowship, a copy was delivered to every home on the island. This project was launched in Town Church, where John Elliston, one of the first members of the Guernsey branch of NYLC forty years earlier, was now rector. This outreach and John's wider ministry were recognized by the media company Guiton Group, who presented John with the Guernsey Ambassador of the Year Award. A revised edition of the book, for ongoing use after the crucial date had passed, was published in 2000 under the title *The Man who Made the Millennium*.

As the new millennium dawned, John was booked to go into hospital for a routine operation. This was completed on 31 January 2000, and at first all appeared to be well. However, three weeks later he developed what the surgeon described as the worst post-operation infection he had ever seen and was rushed back into hospital. Joyce was deeply distressed by John's failure to respond and after one hospital visit told their son Stephen that he might never see his Dad again. But God had other ideas, and after intensive treatment John returned home and was able to resume his preaching seven weeks later.

In March 2000 *Does God Believe in Atheists?* was duly published and took the Christian world by storm. The unique combination of philosophy, anthropology, geology and the life sciences was thoroughly researched and presented. It was a masterful and comprehensive defence of belief in God and a classic on the subject. John was already a widely respected author and speaker with a God-given ability to defend the Christian faith in a clear and concise way, but this was something else. 'Even by his normal standards of excellence and clarity, this work is a tour de force,' wrote the Rev. Dr Sinclair B. Ferguson in the foreword to the book. It came to be known as 'the big book', and the following year it was voted Christian Book of the Year at the UK Christian Book awards. However, not everyone grasped the title of the book. On one occasion John heard the book referred to as *Does God Believe in Anaesthetics?* At his next event he shared this with the audience and said he hoped that nothing he said would put them to sleep!

The impact of the book was such that John had no doubt where his future ministry lay. Neither did he doubt the enormity of the challenge. He mapped out his first twelve objectives, which soon became thirty, and the 'Popular Christian Apologetics Project' (PCAP) was born.

One reaction to 'the big book' came from an engineer and lecturer who said that John's detailed research would easily qualify him for a doctorate. Early in 2001 Pacific International University, which has twin bases in the USA and Canada and twelve seminaries throughout the Pacific Rim, awarded John a Doctor of

Divinity degree for his contribution to Christian apologetics, with particular reference to his research for *Does God Believe in Atheists?* Graduation day was 8 June 2001 in Glendale, California. Both John and Joyce attended the ceremony and he delivered the Graduation Address taking the subject of 'Grace'. He told the audience:

> Grace distinguishes Christianity from all of man's own religious ideas, with their emphasis on human merit and effort. This is why unregenerate man hates the gospel. It insults his intelligence, strikes at his pride and exposes his wickedness. Only when God graciously intervenes is the enemy overcome.

This was to be the start of an increased interest in John's PCAP work and many new doors opened for him. He received invitations to speak at universities, including Oxford and Cambridge, as well as in the United States and South Africa. There was also an increase in radio and television opportunities, both in the UK and abroad.

On 11 September 2001 the most murderous and devastating terrorist attack in history took place in New York City. The twin towers, those beautiful and elegant buildings that graced the skyline of Manhattan, were reduced to millions of tons of rubble and became a gruesome graveyard for thousands of people. In Britain, *The Times* newspaper called it 'a tragedy that stretched human powers of understanding to breaking point'. People all around the world were asking the same question: 'Where was God on that day?' John was asked, 'Where was God when religious fanatics killed all those people?' He replied, 'Exactly where he was when religious fanatics killed his Son Jesus Christ — in complete control of everything that happened.'

John felt challenged to provide a more detailed answer to this question, and in January 2002 *Where was God on September 11?* was published. In the booklet he told of an American Airlines passenger who gave a stewardess a Christian tract on the day before the terrorist attack. She told him it was the sixth tract of this kind that she had received recently and asked, 'What does God want from me?' The passenger replied, 'Your life', and explained the need for her to get right with God by trusting Jesus Christ. Less than twenty-four hours later she was on the first plane to crash into the World Trade Centre. God promises, 'You will seek me and find me when you seek me with all your heart' (Jeremiah 29:13). But, as John pointed out, this gracious invitation has a closing date: 'Seek the LORD while he may be found; call on him while he is near' (Isaiah 55:6). The steward-ess had no idea that her closing date was a matter of hours away and her remarkable story is a sobering reminder that nobody can afford to play fast and loose with God and assume that they can respond to him at their own convenience.

John's first PCAP objective was to complete a public presentation against atheism, giving the reason for the hope of Christianity, in every county in the United Kingdom. As he began to do this, he could see a clear need for more written resources to present the truth to unbelievers and to arm twenty-first-century Christians for the fight against atheism. Having started to write a small book in 1997, which had eventually become 'the big book', John decided to return to the small book, and in 2002 *Is God Past his Sell-By Date?* was published.

Because there are countless ideas of who or what God is, John started the book by clarifying that the God of the Bible is a unique, personal, plural, spiritual, eternally self-existent, transcendent, immanent, omniscient, immutable, holy, loving Being, the Creator and Ruler of the entire universe and the Judge of all mankind. It is this God that he wrote about in a masterful way, challenging the sceptic and the atheist. This God has no 'sell-by date' — and ten very different people contributed their personal stories to the book to testify to the living reality of the God of the Bible. It is to this God that John has entrusted his life, his marriage, his ministry and his future.

This book was quickly followed by the booklet *Evolution — Fact or Fiction?*, which tackled the theory of evolution, dismantling the assumption that such a powerful and comprehensive idea must be true. In it John explained that the universe exists to reflect the glory of its Creator, whose sovereign will is the original cause of all things. Creation is by nature miraculous, and miracles cannot be addressed in scientific terms. There were no eyewitnesses and no cameras. There were no precedents. It wasn't a repetition of something that had happened before. The only way to come to a right understanding of creation is by faith. The booklet is a brilliant defence of divine creation, which the Christian believes with complete confidence because the Word of God tells him it happened.

This was to be the start of non-stop writing in support of the PCAP project. John was now increasingly involved in evangelistic apologetics, rather than in traditional evangelism, and his ministry had undergone a radical change.

Meanwhile, on 30 April 2003, Christian Ministries was brought to an end by a unanimous decision from the three evangelists involved. For twenty-three years CM had been the 'umbrella' over the ministries of the three men and had, by the grace of God, made a considerable impact on the work of the gospel both in the UK and overseas. In the final issue of their newsletter *Communication*, the administrator, Mervyn Snow, wrote:

> As Board members we have counted it a great privilege to stand with these men for the past 23 years. We are so thankful that the Lord has kept them unflinchingly faithful in proclaiming God's word for today's world. We wholeheartedly commend them to your prayers in the coming days.

John looks back on CM with great fondness and enjoyed the warmest of fellowship with his two close friends Peter Anderson and Derek Cleave.

7

Let battle commence

By now John had been joined by Howard Williams on all his PCAP tours. Howard became his driver and handled all the practical arrangements for each site. In particular he took complete charge of all the growing resources that played such a significant part in extending John's vital ministry far beyond the meetings themselves. John had never known a time in his life when so many people were openly attacking the Christian faith. 'Twenty years ago,' he said, 'it would have been unthinkable to have London buses with "There is probably no God" written on the side.' He knew the need to battle against these attacks was great, and so was his determination. What started off as one large book had already grown to include many smaller books, booklets, CDs and DVDs, supplies of which were taken with them on each tour. Many hundreds of

John and Joyce

John and Joyce on their wedding day
— 22 August 1957 at Holy Trinity Church, Guernsey
(p.26)

The newly-weds
walking on Guernsey

John and Joyce celebrate their Golden Wedding on 22 August 2007
(p.105)

The Blanchard family

Joyce with her five boys in their home in Weston-Super-Mare in 1970

Front row, left to right: Stephen, Michael, Andrew

Back row, left to right: Christopher and Timothy

The five Blanchard boys at the family home in Banstead in 1997

Left to right : Stephen, Michael, Andrew, Christopher and Timothy

MWE and Christian Ministries

A group of MWE evangelists in the 1970s (pp. 37-51)

Left to right: Derek Cleave, Dave Pope, Peter Anderson, Ian Coffey and John Blanchard

Easter 2003 — the final Christian Ministries event at Brunel Manor, Torquay
(pp. 78-9)

The 'ABC of Evangelism'
Left to right: Peter **A**nderson, John **B**lanchard and Derek **C**leave

Some events in a busy diary...

While speaking at the Orkney International Science Festival in September 2003, John took the world's shortest commercial flight from the islands of Westray to Papa Westray, which took less than 2 minutes!

John was invited to present 25 copies of *Does God believe in Atheists?* to Liverpool's Central Library in May 2004
(p.87)

Some events in a busy diary...

John and Howard displaying trophies from the Christian Golfers' Conference in Westport, Republic of Ireland, in May 2006

John speaking on *Has Science got rid of God?* at Gateacre Community Comprehensive School, Liverpool, in 2007 (p.103)

John shared the ministry with Bob Dickie at a Ukraine conference organized by Evangelical Press in 2007. *Left to right*: Bob Dickie, Senior Pastor at Berean Baptist Church, Grand Blanc; John; Pastor Alexandr Schmidt (translator); and Jaroslav Viazovski, Assistant Pastor from Belarus and the conference chairman (p.104)

John talking to students in October 2008 at the Royal College of Surgeons, Dublin, Republic of Ireland, on the subject 'Where is God when things go wrong?' (p.103)

Some events in a busy diary...

John at the 2010 Christian
Resources Exhibition being
presented with the 'Resource
of the Year' award for *Why on
Earth did Jesus come?*
(p.118)

John with Rick
Denham at the
FIEL Conference in
Agua de Madeiros,
Portugal,
in October 2010
(p.127)

John recording a
45-minute interview
at Inverness TV
in June 2011

John in Mantova, Italy,
in September 2011
with Pastor Andrea Artioli
(p.139)

Albania

John speaking at Fier Public Library, Albania, in April 2006 (p.92)

John speaking to students in
Vlora, Albania,
in March 2007
(pp. 103-4)

John delivering new titles
in the Albanian language
to Will Niven, the British
missionary co-ordinating
Project Albania
(p.112)

The USA in April 2011

John speaking from the 'clean pages' in
Christ Community Church, Albuquerque,
New Mexico (p.129)

John with Pastor Bob Brown
and Howard
in Christ Community Church (p.129)

A presentation dinner
at The Reserve,
Lake Keowee, South
Carolina, in John's
honour, organized
by Trey Lee and Dr
Buddy Thompson
(p.136)

Left to right:
Howard,
Trey's wife Cynda,
John, Buddy
and Trey

John and Howard point to the locker
at The Reserve, Lake Keowee (p.136)

John with his hosts, Dr Bill and Mrs Lou Anne
Harper, Jackson, Mississippi (p.134)

John, with Senior Pastor Harry Reeder and his
wife Cindy, at Briarwood Presbyterian Church,
Birmingham, Alabama (p.134)

John with his good friend and EP Director,
Pastor Bob Dickie, at Berean Baptist Church,
Grand Blanc, Michigan (p.137)

miles on the road, hours of packing and unpacking of materials, plus a succession of late nights, all added up to a lot of hard work. John says of Howard:

> He does all of this cheerfully and efficiently. He has become a very close friend and a valuable part of the project. Best of all, he shares my joy in hearing of those who come to faith in Christ. He has a servant's heart and it is no exaggeration to say that by his service he has added ten years to my ministry.

Fortunately Howard is also devoted to golf and so the two men are able to compare their rounds of golf, hole by hole, without driving anyone else to distraction! John is a member of Cuddington Golf Club, Surrey, and has taken every opportunity to distribute free copies of his books to fellow golf-club members. He visits 'eighteen friends' there every Wednesday morning, come what may. The detailed analysis of this weekly visit is then shared with Howard, who gives the necessary congratulations or commiserations as the circumstances demand.

John invited Howard to the annual Christian Golfers' Conference at Westport, Co. Mayo, in the Republic of Ireland in 2001. It was there in 2003 that Howard's wife, Marlene, met Joyce for the first time. They became firm friends and discovered a shared passion for the *Daily*

Telegraph crossword. Their first task every morning, after a hurried breakfast, was to dash into town to purchase two copies of the newspaper. Then they would head for a favourite coffee shop and settle down to start the day's crossword. Later, the men would return from a day's golf, full of stories of fantastic drives and brilliant putts — while Joyce and Marlene would happily debate whether '21 across' was an anagram or not.

One very important feature of PCAP has been the translation of John's books into other languages. This has greatly extended the scope of the project. It is said that five languages (English, French, Spanish, Russian and Chinese) can, between them, reach almost the entire world population. EP has published many of his books in all five of these languages — and some in over forty other languages, too. The one which has been translated into more languages than any other is *Ultimate Questions* and John signed away royalty rights to the booklet to help further its distribution.

In 2003 a Burmese translation was published. David Mang Sum, Founder and Director of the Christian Missionary Training Centre in Mangan, Myanmar, said, 'This booklet is one of the best available in Burmese. It will be very effective to reach educated and uneducated people. The message of the book will surely lead even atheists to know the living God.'

The same year 160,000 copies of the Russian translation were delivered to Moscow, St Petersburg and Yaraslav. A group of Christians wrote:

> We are so glad the *Ultimate Questions* finally arrived. Our prayers and hopes have been answered. This book is the best one for all the people who write to us for the first time. Many of them have not a clue of who God is or what faith is. We recommend this book to everyone who is working in the field of evangelization, spreading the good news as our Lord told us to.

Doug Crutchley, a good friend of John's, personally distributed 7,000 copies of the booklet on the streets of Cape Town in South Africa, bringing his total to 40,000 distributed over the previous seven years. At this point the extraordinary demand for the booklet resulted in a total multi-language reprint of over 500,000 copies. Digital recordings were also made in Cantonese, Mandarin and Hokkien, for the benefit of those unable to read, and John was greatly encouraged by the enterprise of the Christians who completed this work.

In November 2003 the annual conference for Russian-speaking pastors was switched at the last minute from Belarus to Poland. John was invited to speak at the conference with Gordon Keddie, pastor of a church in Pennsylvania, and John Rubens. The three men landed in Warsaw and then John Rubens drove the other two on the long and difficult journey to the conference centre. The roads were totally unfamiliar and in the darkness the driver did his best to find the way. He received no help from his two 'back-seat drivers', who enjoyed making constant references to his lack of driving and navigation skills.

When they finally arrived they discovered that the conference centre was a young people's camp and they were housed in wooden huts surrounded by woodland. It was extremely cold and the huts were barely warm enough to sleep in. John found he was sharing a hut with John Rubens, the car driver, who by that time was planning some form of retaliation against his ungrateful passenger. The next morning John Rubens went into the freezing cold bathroom and decided not to use the icy-cold shower. He then reported back to John that the shower had 'plenty of power' and awaited the outcome. He was not disappointed. Two minutes later John went into the shower and turned it on full blast. His screams were enough to wake up the whole camp! The men became part of 'the great unwashed' that week, but enjoyed an extremely good conference with pastors from Poland, Russia and the Ukraine.

Early 2004 saw the end of John's first year as an independent evangelist. In April his goal to take the *Does*

God Believe in Atheists? presentation to every county in the United Kingdom was complete. This journey through England, Scotland, Wales and Northern Ireland had been quite an odyssey, but so much remained to be done. His mind was filled with a great number of things that needed to be written, recorded and filmed. As a result two more titles were published and both met very specific needs.

John was increasingly disturbed that so many Christians seemed unable to defend the integrity and authority of the Bible. The Bible has always been viciously attacked, and millions of copies have been burned over the centuries. Translators have been imprisoned, and some were even executed. Yet there has never been a book in the whole of history that has had such a powerful impact for good on the lives of millions of people all over the world. Why all this hostility and hatred for this particular book and no other? *Why Believe the Bible?* addressed this issue and dealt with the accuracy and reliability of the biblical text. It also examined the Bible's astonishing unity, reliable prophecies and the strength of its claims.

The second book was written in answer to the increasingly prevalent belief that science had replaced God. Its aim was to answer the question posed in the title, *Has Science got Rid of God?* John did not underestimate the size of this daunting task. He is not a scientist and did

not study science at school. He told the story of a judge
in America who imposed a ninety-nine-year sentence
on a man who appeared before him. The man looked
up at him pleadingly and said, 'But, sir, I'm already
eighty-one years old.' 'Well,' said the judge, 'why don't
you go away and do as much as you can?' John said he
felt a bit like that when faced with this huge topic.
However, over fifty years of serious study, reading and
research into the subject have provided him with
enough expert information and analysis to be able to
demonstrate that God is the source of all true science.
The book showed how modern science was triggered
by world-class scientists who believed in God, creation
and the Bible. Many of today's outstanding scientists
are also committed Christians and see no conflict
between their science and their faith.

John is always quick to point out that he does not set
up science in one corner and Christianity in another, as
though they were in opposition. In one of his apologetics talks he says, 'Hear me carefully — true science and
true Christianity are friends, not enemies.' He has the
highest respect for science, but is always quick to point
out that it cannot answer life's biggest questions, or
meet its deepest needs. He says that true science will go
honestly and openly where the evidence leads. It is
humble and is prepared to make a statement and then,
many years later, to adjust this in the light of new

discoveries. When we come to the miraculous and to spiritual issues, the best that science can do is to provide secondary evidence that supports biblical truth. John states very clearly that if there is a scientific statement which contradicts a statement in the Bible, the scientific statement is always wrong and the Bible is always right.

In May 2004 John visited the famous city of Liverpool and preached at the 175th anniversary of the Liverpool City Mission. During this visit the city's Central Library accepted twenty-five copies of *Does God Believe in Atheists?* — one for each of their branches.

In the same year 4,000 copies of *Ultimate Questions* in English and Greek were distributed at the Olympic Games in Athens and a brilliantly presented reprint of John's book *Whatever Happened to Hell?* was published. One reviewer called it 'as exhaustive a treatment of the biblical doctrine of hell as is ever likely to be written in our contemporary culture'.

Because of his move into apologetics, John thought his days of ministering at Bible conventions were over, but he received four invitations in that year. The first was to the Bournemouth and Poole Bible Convention, where John looked at the Bible's teaching on the providence of God, the deity and humanity of Christ, the transformation when Christians get to heaven and the believer's responsibility to be actively involved in witnessing to the relevance and power of the gospel. In addition to preaching, John was able to take part in an hour-long radio broadcast on Hope FM, one of many media opportunities that year.

From there he went to the Midlands, to the Donnington Bible Convention, where he spoke on the book of James and also did a live telephone interview for BBC Radio Jersey.

The third convention was in Longhorsley, a village north of Newcastle, where a university student came to faith in Christ after the first day's ministry.

The fourth invitation was to the Scottish Northern Convention, where John was delighted to share the opening sessions with his long-time friend Alistair Begg, who had moved from Scotland in 1983 to minister in Cleveland, Ohio, in the USA. John also spoke to the faculty and students at Highland Theological College, of which he is a governor.

While on a PCAP tour in Plymouth, John was interviewed for Straighttalk TV, which aimed to get evangelical content shown on one of the channels open on Sky TV. He was also invited to be a guest on *The Julian Worricker Show* on BBC Radio 5 Live. This was a live interview followed by a listeners' phone-in which proved to be a very lively session. After the event one of the warmest emails came from a sceptic who disagreed with virtually everything John had said but appreciated the way he had said it.

John was able to speak freely about questions arising from *Why Believe the Bible?* on Radio KCLR in the Republic of Ireland. Then came an unexpected invitation to speak on the *Jeremy Vine Show* on BBC Radio 2, triggered by BBC Television's decision to screen *Jerry Springer – the Opera*. This was followed by an invitation from the BBC to be interviewed by local radio stations on Easter Sunday morning, and he talked to presenters from Oxford, Cornwall, Coventry and Warwickshire, Greater Manchester, York, Berkshire, Bristol, Northampton, Jersey and Guernsey.

John also writes letters to the press, and on one occasion the *Daily Telegraph* printed a letter from him in response to the fact that atheists had asked to be included in BBC Radio 4's *Thought for the Day*. This is a short slot where religious contributors give a brief and uplifting message to help encourage the listener. John said he would be very interested to know what atheists could possible contribute to this when they believe that 'we begin as a fluke, we live as a farce and we end as fertilizer'.

Nothing gives John greater joy than hearing how God has graciously used his ministry and his books to bring men and women into faith in Christ. He frequently funds supplies of books and other resources for anyone

who cannot afford to buy them. In April 2004 a lady
drove two-and-a-half hours to a meeting in Matlock to
tell him that she had begun reading *Does God Believe in
Atheists?* as an atheist and had trusted in Christ when
she was two-thirds of the way through the book. He
received many more emails telling him of similar
testimonies, including one from a Greek young lady
whose father had found faith in Christ just before he
died by reading the Greek translation of *Ultimate
Questions.*

8
Light in a dark place

With the fall of the Iron Curtain, the Soviet Union's domination of Eastern Europe ended and the doors were now wide open for the spread of Christianity. This provided yet another exciting opening for John. EP arranged for him to speak at conferences in several Eastern European countries, including Poland, Romania and Ukraine over the next few years. These events left a lasting impression on him and he was deeply moved by the total commitment and dedication of the Christians and their pastors.

One country in particular caught his attention. Under Soviet Communism, Albania had become the world's first atheist state and its leaders were determined to eradicate all traces of Christianity. Churches were closed down; Bibles were destroyed; the word 'God' was removed from the language, and Christians were punished for their faith. After the fall of the Iron Curtain the country was open to all manner of religions and cults.

When John first visited Albania, he spoke at the Way of Peace Church in Lushnje. The next day found him in Patos, and then at a larger town called Fier. This visit had an enormous effect on John. He was deeply moved by the faith and love for the gospel shown by the Christians he met. They had a great concern for the lost and yet had few resources. He immediately launched 'Project Albania', which aimed to raise £19,000 to pay for the translation and printing of some of his books. One of his interpreters, Florenc Mene, had been praying for three years for *Does God Believe in Atheists?* to be translated into Albanian. So John widened the scope of his project and the translation was completed. This was the start of annual visits, which still continue today, giving John the privilege of sharing the good news of the gospel with largely non-Christian audiences.

In December 2004 the devastating tsunami in the Indian Ocean led to countless people asking where God was when this happened. A letter in the *Daily Telegraph* asked, 'On the abundant available evidence does it not seem that if there is or was a God, it is now malevolent or dead?' This and many similar reactions in the media spurred John to update *Where was God on September 11?*

and in March 2005 *Where is God when Things go Wrong?* was published in the UK, with a separate edition in the United States. This tackled an extremely emotive subject and answered a very difficult question. John did not sidestep the serious issues involved, but tackled them head-on. He said that headline-making atrocities are wake-up calls, warning us that evil and suffering are real, life is brief and fragile, and death is certain.

Many people saw 9/11 as God's judgement against America, but Jesus made it clear in the Bible that we have no warrant for saying that. Rather than accusing God of appalling cruelty, we should accept that in his infinite wisdom he withdrew his protective hand and allowed this to take place for purposes that are beyond our limited human understanding, except that of seeing it as a warning of the judgement that awaits all who reject his claims. The fact that 'All have sinned and fall short of the glory of God' (Romans 3:23) means that if he were to eliminate the whole of humanity at this moment neither his justice nor his righteousness would be compromised. John continued, 'You are alive at this moment only because, for the time being, God does not treat us as our sins deserve.' At the end of the booklet John gave 'the best news you will ever hear' about turning from sin and trusting Jesus Christ as Saviour, which brings forgiveness of sins, peace with God and eternity in heaven.

John's many visits to South Africa, arranged by the Alpha and Omega Trust and Christian Book Discounters, were now centred on his apologetics project, and the need for its message was very evident. In 2005 his fifth visit was a great encouragement to him. Attendances were beyond all his expectations and events included evangelism workshops, lectures at the three largest universities and radio and television interviews.

In Durban he spoke at a specially called meeting of biology teachers and senior students. The South African government had decreed that in two years' time evolution *must* be taught at senior school level. John exposed the flaws in neo-Darwinism and confirmed the solid base for biblical creationism.

He was once again encouraged by hearing how his books had brought people to a saving knowledge of Jesus Christ. A soldier gave his life to Christ during his time on the front line in the war in Namibia while reading *What in the World is a Christian?*, a book that John wrote back in 1975. Several people in the same church became Christians when they read *Ultimate Questions*. One of South Africa's most prominent artists found faith while reading *Does God Believe in Atheists?* and another man told John that he began reading the book as an atheist, was an agnostic at the halfway point and a Christian at the end.

John returned home with very mixed feelings: happy to be going home to his beloved Joyce but sorry to leave a truly great country with such a massive spiritual potential.

Later that year John visited Zambia for the first time and addressed 300 students in Kabwata Baptist Church, Lusaka, led by Pastor Conrad Mwebe, a man passionate about the gospel. John found the visit to be a challenging eye-opener. Twenty years of rampant socialism had led to terrible deprivation. Over 65% of the population were HIV positive, and life expectancy was just thirty-six years. Yet in this desperate setting the light and hope of the gospel were shining out. In Kitwe the American pastor Phil Hunt and a dedicated team were preaching, teaching, running a school and an orphanage, and reaching out to hundreds of students at Copperbelt University. As a result of this visit, *Ultimate Questions* was translated into two Zambian languages, Bemba and Nyanja.

In July 2006, 15,000 copies of the booklet were given out to American military personnel serving in Iraq. In April 2007 a young South Korean murdered thirty of his fellow students and others at Virginia Tech University in Blacksburg, Virginia. This was an appalling tragedy, and a local church distributed 4,500 copies of *Where is God when Things go Wrong?* at the memorial service and in the course of their ongoing support for those affected.

John wrote a new evangelistic booklet in May 2006 entitled *Is Anybody out There?*, and a CD of one of his presentations on that subject was produced for the PCA project. This booklet raised and answered questions that have been asked down the centuries: 'Why am I here? What is the meaning of life? Why should I believe anything? What happens when I die? Is there anything beyond our universe?' John had worked with the publishers, EP, for some time to 'pull out all the stops' on this publication. The result was a superb booklet, illustrated with stunning graphics, attractive to the non-Christian and an excellent outreach tool for Christians. It showed the God of the Bible to be the only answer to man's need for truth, identity, love, security and forgiveness. It also dismantled the popular idea that all religions lead eventually to God.

In the same year EP published another book by John, but it was something completely different. Ever since he became a Christian John has collected quotes from a variety of sources, ranging from preachers and politicians to scientists and sceptics. He finds these quotations fascinating and addictive. He says they sharpen his thinking, broaden his perspective and often shed light on old truths. Over the years he simply stored them away, but in 1984 he compiled a treasury of quotations, which was published under the title *Gathered Gold*, and this was later followed by two further volumes. Finally, in 2006 he added over 1,000 new quotations, and the full collection, containing over 16,000 quotes on 600 subjects, was reissued in a new hard-backed volume, *The Complete Gathered Gold*. The quotations cover a wide range of topics: some devotional and some practical; some serious and some amusing; some challenging and some reassuring. Together they form an absolute treasury of teaching, advice and guidance.

John has always appreciated any opportunity to speak in universities and to bring the message of the gospel to young people. That year he was invited by the Christian Union to speak at University College, London, the third oldest university in England, after Oxford and Cambridge. It is proud of its secular roots and the fact that the Christian message rarely gets a look in. This presents a great challenge to the college Christian Union, and John was only too grateful to take up their invitation and to lift the Saviour high. At least one third of the audience were not Christians, and much encouraging feedback was received after the event, including a comment from one student who said it was 'the best talk I have heard for five years'.

The PCAP had now expanded to include lectures on the subjects of John's new publications: *Has Science got*

Rid of God?, *Is God Past his Sell-By Date?*, *Where is God when Things go Wrong?* and *Is Anybody out There?* Each event included a forty-five-minute talk followed by an open question-and-answer session and then a final fifteen-minute summary and challenge. John faced hundreds of different questions and gave both scientific and scriptural answers. Not knowing what will be asked, or whether there will any antagonism, is a risk he is prepared to take in order to share biblical truth with everyone he can.

On one occasion an atheist asked whether he would be sent to hell for stealing a Mars bar from Tesco, which he said would be a bit harsh compared with the crimes of Adolf Hitler. 'Yes,' replied John, 'because that is not the only crime you have committed. Jesus said the first and great commandment is to love the Lord your God with all your heart, soul, mind and strength. That's the trouble — not the Mars bar.'

By now he was receiving a constant stream of invitations to talk on these subjects and was arranging several tours each year, accompanied by Howard. These included return visits to venues throughout the UK and the Republic of Ireland, where he had made many lasting and valuable friendships.

In 2005 the Northern Ireland tour included an invitation to join in the annual Baptist Men's Day Golf

Tournament in Magheralin. This was no hardship to John and Howard, who always pack their golf clubs when going on tour, just in case... There was an after-dinner opportunity for John to share the gospel with over eighty men and to distribute gospel literature. An added bonus was meeting a man who had found faith in Christ while reading *Ultimate Questions*.

John's next apologetics tour in Scotland began in East Kilbride, where he was greatly encouraged by the testimony of a young American woman to the relevance of the gospel when Hurricane Katrina hit her home town of New Orleans.

A visit to Wales was next on the PCAP agenda and this began in Cardiff and then moved to Llanelli. John then took part in a live interview on BBC Radio 2's *Jeremy Vine Show* along with Terry Waite, one-time special envoy of the Archbishop of Canterbury. He appreciated this opportunity to discuss the gospel and the need to proclaim it boldly. This was followed by an apologetics presentation at the local university. The following day John and Howard completed the long journey to Bangor University, where the main Arts Theatre was full to capacity, with students sitting in the aisles. The next day saw them in the Grove Theatre in Aberystwyth University, where the question-and-answer session was so animated that the caretaker eventually had to call 'time' and ask everyone to leave the building! The final visit was to Newport and ended a delightful tour, meeting many friends and making new ones, with the added bonus of nearly 200 people asking for a free copy of *Right with God.*

In September 2005 both John and Joyce visited New Mexico and, after he had preached at five services and before they headed for Georgia, they fulfilled a lifelong ambition to visit the Grand Canyon in Arizona. Nothing had prepared them for this staggering and overwhelming sight — 277 miles long, 18 miles wide and reaching 5,000 feet down to the Colorado River. John spoke later of the thoughts that had gone through his mind as he gazed at this testimony to God's awesome power. Despite its size, the Grand Canyon is merely a scratch on the surface of a planet orbiting around a star a million times its size, within one of 100,000 million galaxies in the known universe. That all this was brought into being by the spoken word of God is beyond our understanding and is a towering testimony to his creative power. John also thought of another vast canyon, the 'great gulf' referred to in the Bible and which is fixed between heaven and hell. It reminded him of the urgent responsibility he has as a Christian to share the gospel of Jesus Christ with those who do not know him, telling them of the Saviour who alone can rescue them from sin and from hell.

When John began his full-time Christian service back in 1962 it never entered his head that writing books would become part of his evangelism. But by now this was a major part of his work and a great extension of his ministry, and one that God was using in an amazing way. The titles of his PCAP booklets were all vitally important questions which demanded answers, and John used his unique, God-given skills to provide those answers.

The demand for *Ultimate Questions* continued to rise beyond anything he had ever imagined. A further reprint of 411,000 copies arrived, and these included 23,500 in English, 23,000 in Albanian, 20,000 in Spanish, 20,000 in Russian, 11,000 in French, 10,000 in Afrikaans and 5,000 in each of another sixteen languages, including, for the first time, Bemba (Zambia) and Xhosa (South Africa).

Although he did not preach in Holland until 2007, there was a lot of interest in his work in that country and *Why believe the Bible?* was published in Dutch by EP along with a Dutch translation of *The Beatitudes Today* published by Day One.

In the same year EP published a new fortieth-anniversary edition of *Read Mark Learn*, which is still widely used by people for personal Bible reading and by study groups. In addition, the free copies are sent out every year to people from all around the world who write to say that they have found faith in Christ by reading one of John's books.

In 2007 *Can we be Good without God?* was published. In it John looked at the moral dimension that distinguishes human beings from every other species on earth. He considered the question why we seem to be pro-grammed with a moral law which is activated by the conscience. What, he asked, is the deciding factor? Are there any consistent guidelines? At a PCAP lecture on this subject he told the story of a clockmaker who had a magnificent clock on permanent display in the centre of his shop window. Every morning a man stopped outside the window and looked at the clock. This intrigued the clockmaker, and one morning he stepped outside the shop and asked the man why he stopped there every morning. The man told him that he was the timekeeper at the nearby factory and responsible for blowing the hooter that marked the end of each work-ing day. It was very important that the factory closed on time and because his watch didn't keep good time, he synchronized it every morning with the splendid clock in the shop window. 'I don't know how to tell you this,' said the shopkeeper, 'but the clock doesn't work very well either, so I synchronize it every afternoon when the hooter blows at the factory.' In *Can we be Good without God?* John asked, and answered, the most important question: 'Can we ever have a solid and coherent basis for morality unless our world view has God at the very centre of it?'

John is always ready for any invitation to share and defend the gospel. On his north-west PCAP tour that year he received an unexpected invitation to speak on 'Science and Christianity' to 120 senior students at Gateacre Community Comprehensive School, the biggest in Liverpool. The students listened attentively and asked many penetrating questions. Over 100 students took away a free copy of *Has Science got Rid of God?*

In the following year John received an invitation to address the Royal College of Surgeons (RCSI) in Dublin. He was asked by the Christian Union to speak on the subject, 'Where is God when things go wrong?', after which all the free copies of the booklet accompanying the talk were taken.

By early 2007 Project Albania had achieved many of its objectives. The original target of £19,000 had been raised to £21,000, and this meant that 5,000 copies of *Right with God* were added to the seven titles originally selected for translation into Albanian. Further translations, of his latest booklet, *Can we be Good without God?* and a special printing of *Ultimate Questions* were also funded. John was able to make a return visit to the country at this time and to speak to many young people and students in several locations. He enjoyed excellent question-and-answer sessions despite power cuts, which are a daily feature of life in Albania.

In this very busy year John crossed the Atlantic once again, this time with the added delight of Joyce's company, to preach in five states. He also visited Ukraine to speak at one of the conferences organized by EP. This was held in Village Kozin, about an hour's drive from Kiev and originally a Soviet sanatorium. Over 100 pastors, preachers, missionaries, church leaders and their wives were there from Ukraine, Russia, Lithuania and Moldova. John shared the ministry with a very dear friend, Pastor Bob Dickie, senior pastor at Berean Baptist Church, Grand Blanc, Michigan.

In May 2007 John made his first preaching visit to Holland. This was arranged by de Banier, a publishing house founded in 1928, disbanded in World War II, when the Germans took over the printing presses, and then revived in 1948. Over the years, it had issued Dutch versions of five of John's titles and so was extremely keen to meet him in person. He spoke several times a day in five locations and felt it was a special privilege to speak to so many people who were seriously attentive to his ministry.

This same year was to see the publication of a new edition of *How to Enjoy your Bible*. John wrote this book out of two firmly held convictions. The first is that the

Bible is the inspired Word of God, infallible, pure and perfect in every way. He looked at its divine source, its preservation, its relevance and its power to change lives. Secondly, he believes that Christians are meant to enjoy the Bible as a means of enlightenment, enrichment and encouragement. In his experience many Christians seem to fall short of this, finding Bible reading a duty rather than a delight. In the book John enthused about the Bible as the Heavenly Father's chosen means of communication with his children, and therefore priceless and unique. John's earnest desire is for Christians to be enthusiastic about it, to plumb its depths and experience its never-ending riches.

2007 was a very special year for another reason. On 22 August John and Joyce celebrated their Golden Wedding with a delightful train journey through Switzerland. John acknowledged God's gracious hand in bringing someone so very special into his life. Joyce had supported his ministry in such a wonderful, sacrificial way and had cared for their five sons as John's travels took him beyond the UK to Europe, the USA and elsewhere. She was quietly content to be at home and in her own unique way had also been a radiant witness to the Saviour. They agreed that the past fifty years had been a mixture of delights and disappointments, sunshine and shadows, laughter and tears, peaceful days and those filled with painful pressures. Yet through it all they had known God's guiding hand and his unfailing love. Cecil Myers once wrote, 'Successful marriage is always a triangle: a man, a woman and God.' John and Joyce knew this to be true and on their anniversary day they prayed that he would graciously draw them both even closer to himself and to each other.

2008 saw John back on the road again with more PCAP tours. The final meeting of a north-west tour strayed into North Wales (geography is still not John's strong point!) and was held at Ebenezer Baptist Church in Mold. John spoke on the subject 'Where is God when things go wrong?', which obviously touched a nerve with the audience and sparked off many penetrating questions, some of which John had never heard before. On the journey back to Howard's home John realized that this event marked forty-six years in full-time Christian service. It seemed fitting that this milestone should be reached in 'Ebenezer' church, the name meaning, 'Thus far has the LORD helped us.'

That year saw the publication of yet another PCAP booklet, *Where do we Go from Here?* — the question that ultimately concerns every human being on our planet. In this booklet John examined the many views that are held on death and dying before setting out the biblical response to the question. He remembered his first job in the Guernsey Registrar's Office, where he was required to complete death certificates. In particular he recalled completing column 9. The entry in that column was the cause of death. Yet one word would have sufficed for everyone — 'sin'. In the booklet, with compelling honesty, he applied biblical truth to a sensitive subject, giving answers that needed to be said. Once again he demonstrated that he is gifted with intellectual integrity and an ability to hit the mark. This booklet was eagerly received internationally and one pastor in Oklahoma, USA, adopted it as the primary resource tool for evangelism in his city.

While John is always encouraged by hearing from those who have found faith in Christ as a result of reading one of his books, he says he is careful not to 'open the door to pride'. This was reinforced on a visit to Kidderminster, where he completed some research on Richard Baxter, who had an astonishing ministry in that town from 1641–1661. This great man, whose writings have had such a profound impact for over 300 years, said, 'I was but a pen in God's hands, and what praise is due to a pen?'

In October 2008 John returned 'home' to Guernsey fifty years after the original 'Guernsey for God' campaign. He did an interview for BBC Guernsey and spoke at an evangelistic dinner held at La Grande Mare Hotel to celebrate the fiftieth anniversary of the first campaign. John, who will always have a deep love for the people of 'his' island, saw this as a great privilege. He was able to testify to the reality and reliability of the God in whom he placed his entire trust on that memorable night back in 1954.

In February 2009 Day One published *Travel with John Blanchard* in their superb Travel Guide series. These guides follow the stories and travels of well-known Christian preachers and leaders in church history, such as John Bunyan, John Knox, C. H. Spurgeon, William Wilberforce, William Carey and Dr Martyn Lloyd-Jones. When John was asked to become the first 'living' subject of a Travel Guide he refused, feeling inadequate in the company of so many great men of God from the past. He was eventually persuaded to take up the offer, and this started a long and dusty exploration of his loft, wading through many hundreds of items meticulously kept and dating back to the beginning of his ministry fifty-four years ago. This was to be the start of months of research, yet reviewing the past in such detail only served as a humbling reminder of God's amazing providence and goodness. The General Editor of the series, Brian Edwards, a long-time friend and skilled writer, spent endless hours pulling together data, photographs and slides to produce the final product, which contained 150 photographs as well as maps and drawings. John's prayer was that God would graciously use this unexpected publication to his glory.

Later in the year, four counties were visited in one PCAP tour, and a meeting in the south-coast resort of Torquay was a journey down memory lane for John. He passed what was, in 1962, Charterhouse Christian Guest House, the venue of his first-ever message in full-time ministry. Then he saw Teignmouth Baptist Church, the first church in which he preached after arriving in the 'foreign' land of England. This was yet another reminder of God's unerring guidance and grace throughout the past forty-seven years.

John's first visit to South Africa was in 1988, and since then he has had the privilege of preaching hundreds of times in what he calls 'that wonderful country'. He thought that the visit in 2007 would be his last, but Christian Book Discounters, who do a superb work in making good Christian literature available throughout the country, persuaded him to return two years later. This visit was packed with engagements, including a return visit to Seattle Coffee Shop, Hyde Park, for 'Thank God It's Friday'. For ten years TGIF has been a weekly gathering for businessmen and others, and on this occasion John's message was intently received and followed by a very lively question time. From there he visited the Baptist Theological College of South Africa in Randtown, where faculty and students sat for an hour's teaching on the relationship between science and Christianity. The principal then abandoned the usual morning schedule to allow for a further hour's teaching and a challenging question-and-answer time.

One event at Blairgowrie had an unusual format, and one that was a first for John. After 100 people had finished the first course of a superb breakfast, service was suspended while he delivered a 'full-blown message on death and the afterlife', after which the main course was served.

At Johannesburg he shared an apologetics conference called 'Thinking Connected' with Ranald Macaulay, Francis Schaeffer's son-in-law, who co-ordinated the work of Christian Heritage in Cambridge. He flew to the Eastern Cape (his first time in that area) for further engagements, including two sessions of a conference organized by Dumisani Theological Institute.

Another flight, to the Western Cape, brought more superb opportunities. He spoke at three lunch-time meetings organized by City Partnerships in hotels in Cape Town and Somerset West. This was followed by an exhilarating meeting with university students in Stellenbosch, who provided 'the most alert audience' he had ever had. A five-hour round trip to the Klein Karoo town of Montagu saw him address two one-hour morning sessions. More meetings followed in Plum-stead, Bellville and Goodwood, where a man told him that he had been so inspired by reading the first edition of *How to Enjoy your Bible* that he had read the Bible from cover to cover every year for the past twenty years. John was delighted to return to speak at the Bible Institute in Kalk Bay, where he was told that in 1991 one of the lecturers had sent a copy of *Ultimate Questions* to every head of state in the world.

His last day in South Africa began at St James Church, Kenilworth, where he had first preached twenty-one years ago, and this provided a wonderful and memorable climax to the tour. Before leaving for the flight home he rode up Table Mountain for a panoramic view over the Western Cape and quietly thanked God for his enabling grace throughout his many visits to this wonderful part of the world.

In December 2009 John made his third visit to Albania and described it as an 'eye-opener'. The capital city of Tirana was now bursting with new life and awash with Western features and ideas. When he asked his host for the Albanian mind-set he was told they 'had a hard time with sin'. They understood it only in terms of 'big' sins, such as murder, violent robbery and child abuse, but had no concern for 'little' sins. Yet, as John says, there are no little sins because there is no little God to sin against. Even the smallest sin is an affront to the majesty and glory of our great God.

In Albania materialism was in overdrive and one pastor told John that its effect on young people meant that they were more confused than any previous teenage population. In stark contrast, John spent his last day in an area less than three hours from Tirana where countless people did not earn enough to buy daily basics such as bread and milk. This was still the second poorest country in Europe and had been further affected by a huge exodus of people. It is called 'a country surrounded by itself', as so many Albanians live in neighbouring states – 600,000 in Greece, 400,000 in Italy, 1,000,000 in Kosovo and others in Macedonia and elsewhere.

This state of affairs has influenced Project Albania. So too has the very small number of evangelical churches in the country and the fact that a survey showed that 65% of residents are classed either as atheist or agnostic. On this visit John was able to share his 'literature vision' with twenty-five church leaders and the question-and-answer session continued long into the afternoon. The next day a crowded youth meeting heard John speak on 'Creation versus Evolution', with free copies of *Evolution: Fact or Fiction?* being offered to everyone. John was also able to meet up with Will Niven, the British missionary co-ordinating Project Albania. This visit saw the publication of *Does God Believe in Atheists?* and *Has Science got Rid of God?* in Albanian.

Christmas has always been a special time of year for John and Joyce, especially when they were blessed with seven beautiful grandchildren. However, John feels that the real meaning of the season has become progressively more clouded by great sentimentality and so many other things that are totally unconnected to the first Christmas. He recalls going into a card shop to search for a retirement card and having difficulty in finding one because the shop was full of Christmas cards. 'There is nothing surprising about that,' said John, 'but this was September and still British Summer Time. At this rate the herald angels will need suntan lotion!'

Not surprisingly, he decided to add another booklet to his apologetics collection. In *Why on Earth did Jesus Come?* he looked at the real reason for the celebration, which was the birth of a Jewish baby boy in Bethlehem over 2,000 years ago. Seventy billion babies have been born into this world, so what was so special about this one? John explained that this birth was unique, not because the baby was born in a cattle shed, but because the child in the feeding trough was the King on the throne of the universe. On the first Christmas Day (and we do not know the actual date) the creator, sustainer and provider of the entire universe became a man. After hundreds of years of imperfect prophets, priests and kings, the Messiah who had been promised throughout the Old Testament was finally here.

John once again recalled his work in the registrar's office of Guernsey. Everyone on that tiny island knew when a baby was due, and the birth would be registered within thirty days of the baby's arrival. Yet one of many birth announcements concerning the baby born in Bethlehem was made in the Bible 700 years *before* he was born. Then, all those years later, the angels brought good news to a group of shepherds on a hillside. The waiting was over and God had kept his promise.

John said that the miracle of Christmas is not a pregnant virgin, a birth in a stable, a visit from angels, or gifts from wise men. It is the changing of a person's eternal destiny from hell to heaven because of who that baby was and what he did. 'Hear me carefully,' he said when preaching at Grove Chapel, London, in December 2010, 'Christmas is not all about children, family or presents. It is all about sin and our need to be saved from it. This is the one and only message of Christmas. Jesus came into the world to save sinners.' *Why on Earth did Jesus Come?* was published in late 2009 and added to the PCAP library of resources.

John asked for the Albanian translation to be fast-tracked for use at Christmas. This was achieved and he was invited to return to the country for an evangelistic event in December. He preached twice on the Sunday — first in Tirana's Sheraton Hotel and then, in the evening, at the Tirana International Hotel. This crowded venue, with professional musicians and a fine translator, provided a superb backdrop for the message of the incarnation — the real meaning of Christmas.

Around the same time John's thoughts turned to the next important event in the Christian calendar, Easter, and what it commemorates. The Bible claims that Jesus Christ visited this planet over 2,000 years ago, died and then came back to life three days later. Or did he…? Clearly from the atheist's perspective this is not only impossible, but a complete fabrication. Yet the whole of Christianity is based on the fact that Jesus Christ rose from the dead. Everything hinges on his resurrection. Is he alive today? Is he still transforming countless lives across the world, or are millions of people totally deluded?

John answered these questions, and more besides, in his booklet *Jesus: Dead or Alive?* It was written with his usual clarity and thoroughness. He examined the evidence for the resurrection and also the arguments against it. In addition — and this is of the utmost importance — he wrote from personal experience, having had his own life changed by the risen Lord Jesus in 1954 and having known his ongoing, unerring guidance since then.

9

Lonely but not alone

In June 2008 Joyce had several urgent medical tests and it was with great sadness that John received the news that his beloved wife had cancer. She did not ask, 'Why me?' Her response was: 'Why not me?' Through it all her steadfast faith and unwavering Christian witness were clear to doctors and medical staff. She was well cared for at the Royal Marsden Hospital and had surgery and chemotherapy. However, the cancer had spread and soon she was fighting her final battle. She accepted this with the gentle grace that had been a mark of her life as John's greatest supporter and soulmate.

Their times of Bible reading and prayer together became especially precious and the last words of Scripture Joyce heard were: 'Surely goodness and mercy will follow me all the days of my life, and I will dwell in the house of the LORD for ever' (Psalm 23:6). She knew her times were in the Lord's hands and on Wednesday, 17 February 2010, he freed her from all pain by calling her to her eternal home.

On 5 March 2010, under a clear blue sky, John stood shoulder to shoulder with his five sons as Joyce's body was lowered into the grave. It was a poignant moment: one of physical parting and deep sadness, yet also one of great triumph, for she was already with her Lord. Later that day, a wonderful service of thanksgiving was held at which many warm tributes were paid to Joyce. Most importantly, and just as she would have wished, the good news of eternal life in Jesus was preached. The family received over 500 cards, letters and emails expressing sympathy and giving them the assurance of prayerful support.

After fifty-two years of married life John's loss was indescribable. Yet, with God's unfailing presence and help, he was able to pick up the threads of his ministry. With countless friends supporting him in prayer, and in the knowledge that Joyce would wish him to continue to lift the Saviour high, John has continued to follow his PCAP mission statement to do 'as much as I can, as well as I can, for as long as I can'.

While in Albania in December 2009, he was invited to return to preach over the following Easter weekend. He took up the offer and spoke in the city of Tirana at two morning services on Easter Day 2010. He looked at what the consequences would have been if the resurrection of Jesus had never taken place before declaring the Bible's triumphant assertion that it had. Later that day he returned once more to Tirana International Hotel, where he spoke to a large crowd at an evangelistic rally. Many copies of the newly translated *Jesus: Dead or Alive?* were given away. The following day he discussed Project Albania with three key Christian leaders and plans were made for yet more titles to be translated into Albanian, including the major work *Whatever Happened to Hell?*

In May 2010 the annual Christian Resources Exhibition was held at Sandown Park in Surrey and EP encouraged John to attend. He was very surprised to see that his booklet *Why on Earth did Jesus Come?* was on the shortlist for the 'Resource of the Year' award. To his amazement it was voted the winner and John suddenly found himself on his feet giving an acceptance speech. He made it absolutely clear that the greatest thanks were due to the Lord Jesus Christ, 'who is the heartbeat of everything I write'.

Earlier in 2010 the Caribbean island of Haiti was hit by an earthquake, with devastating results. A journalist who surveyed the wreckage said, 'Haiti will need to be completely rebuilt from the ground up.' Over 230,000 people died and 2,000,000 were left homeless. Financial help poured into relief agencies and John's own charitable trust sent 5,000 copies of the French edition of the booklet *Where is God when Things go Wrong?* for use among those who were asking this question.

Later in the year the UK was shocked when a cab driver went on a shooting spree in West Cumbria, killing twelve people before taking his own life. In the days that followed 200 copies of the same booklet were used by Garry Rowcroft, the pastor of Trinity Baptist Church, Maryport, with much prayer that God would use them in this tragic situation.

Richard Dawkins, the British zoologist who was the Charles Simonyi Professor of the Public Understanding of Science at Oxford University, is probably one of the world's best-known atheists today. His book *The God Delusion*, published in 2006, aimed to destroy religion in general and Christianity in particular. In the preface he says, 'If this book works as I intend, religious readers who open it will be atheists when they put it down.' In chapter 2 he says, 'I am attacking God, all gods, anything and everything supernatural, wherever and whenever they have been or will be invented.' This was a nuclear attack on Christianity and written with great authority and academic weight. In 2009 Dawkins wrote *The Greatest Show on Earth*, in which he claimed that all forms of life are a direct consequence of evolution.

In 2010 John's response to this, *Dealing with Dawkins,* was published, and in it he fearlessly defended Christianity. With his usual razor-sharp logic and unique gift for dealing with enormous issues, he showed that, despite his fierce intellect and brilliant scientific mind, Dawkins was wrong in many areas — with regard to science, evolution, religion, morality, God, mankind, the Bible, Christianity and Jesus. Dawkins believes that science has the answers to the big questions about life and has replaced religion in this role. John agrees that science can tell us many things, but not everything. He quoted John Lennox, Professor of Mathematics at the University of Oxford, who said, 'Science can tell you that if you add strychnine to someone's drink it will kill them. But science cannot tell you whether it is morally right or wrong to put strychnine into your grandmother's tea so that you can get your hands on her property.'

John continued, 'Science is the ongoing process of discovering truth in the natural world,' and acknowledged that as such it is to be commended. One of his sons is making considerable strides in a particular discipline in science and John is grateful for that. His son dedicated one of his theses to his parents and neither of them could understand a word of it!

Dawkins rules out a transcendent, divine creator, but in *Dealing with Dawkins* John revealed cracks in his case. Despite Dawkins' passionate belief in atheism, John says he is in denial of its darker side — the most appalling expressions of violent evil in the history of the world were driven by atheism and were not perpetrated in the name of God.

Dawkins admits to there being amazing design in the world, but he is then faced with the question: 'Who designed the designer?' Or, more simply, 'Who made God?' John says the answer depends on which god you mean. Most of this world's gods (and religions) are man-made, and so the answer to the question is obvious — men created them. But the God of the Bible was not created. Everything that had a beginning had a cause, *but God never had a beginning.* At the start of time and space God was already there and the Bible clearly states that he is the eternal God and is from everlasting to everlasting.

One comment addressed to John at a PCAP question-and-answer session was from a person who could not get his head around eternality. John's response was: 'Join the club! Neither can I, but, hear me carefully, that doesn't mean it isn't true, unless I am going to be super-arrogant and say that if I can't get my head around it, it can't be true.' Or, as he frequently says, 'I may not understand it, but I am called to stand under it.' That is one of his guiding principles when studying the Bible and is a measure of his complete trust in the God who has led and sustained him for over fifty years.

John handles hundreds of emails every week, and some are extremely controversial and challenging. The publication of *Dealing with Dawkins* led to an increase in such emails, some of which were personally offensive and extremely unpleasant. Through it all he was supported by an army of prayer partners who pray for him regularly and in this way play a very significant part in his ministry.

John rises very early every morning to start the day with prayer and greatly values the prayers of all the people who uphold him in this way. But in response to the phrase 'Prayer changes things', he says, 'I worry a little bit about that because I don't think prayer changes anything. I think *God* changes things according to his own wisdom.' He explains this by saying that prayer does not activate God's will, as though he were in neutral and needed prompting; neither does it alter God's will, as though he constantly changed his mind. John once read in a Christian magazine about a pastor who had resigned from his role and moved to another job. The report said that he was now 'serving the Lord in an advisory capacity'. This appealed to John's sense of humour. He feels that all too often prayer seems to consist of us telling God what he should do. In actual

fact quite the opposite is true. John says that when God
determines to do something he puts it in the heart of
his chosen people to pray, and then he brings it about.
So God uses our prayers to accomplish his will. In a
wonderful act of condescension he brings us into the
picture and enables us to have an active share in the
working out of his sovereign purposes.

Later in 2010 John added yet another booklet to the
ever-expanding PCAP 'toolkit'. He turned his attention
to the symbol of Christianity — the cross. This is not
only a well-known symbol in churches and on grave-
stones, but is often seen in jewellery and in tattoos. Yet
the cross was a barbaric and gruesome instrument of
execution used for about 1,000 years from the fourth
century BC — a bizarre choice to symbolize Christianity. In the booklet *Why the Cross?* John looked at the
significance of the crucifixion of a man called Jesus
Christ over 2,000 years ago, why it mattered then and
why it still matters today. He explained who Jesus is
and why he died but, more importantly, he looked at
what this means for every individual today and how it
provides the only hope of heaven. John knows from
personal experience that religious observance, services,
rites and rituals can never bridge the gap that sin has
created between God and man. In the booklet he
showed that Jesus was far more than a good role
model: he was a substitute exposed on the cross to

God's rightful anger against sin. In the most amazing act of love ever known he took our place and endured the penalty of sin for us.

John is a very busy man and over the years there have been many invitations he has chosen to reject. However, he says he was once faced with an infinitely more important invitation — from the man who died on a cross and then rose from the dead. This was an invitation from the risen Saviour which he gladly accepted by faith in 1954, and he received the complete assurance of the forgiveness of sins and eternal life in heaven.

He often explains the nature of Christian faith to audiences, and specifically what it involves. He tells them, 'I believe in taking a cold bath before breakfast every morning. There is no better way to start the day than by getting quickly out of bed, running a cold bath and jumping straight in.' This usually produces an audible gasp from the audience — followed by relieved laughter when he adds, 'But I have never had one!' This kind of belief and faith falls a long way short of the faith required in the Bible. John says coming to God in faith involves turning and trusting — and the second is impossible without the first. It is a wholehearted response to Jesus Christ, abandoning all trust in anything else and experiencing a revolution in heart, mind and will.

When *Ultimate Questions* was first published in 1987 no one could have imagined that by 2012 there would be 16,000,000 copies in print in sixty-three languages. A new addition to the *UQ* family is the tiny pocket-sized version which is ideal for personal evangelism and distribution. John continues to be encouraged by the way God is using this booklet and has had many uplifting reports about its recent use.

From Malawi, a pastor thanked him for a gift of 100 copies in Chichewa and said that after he had preached on the booklet four people became Christians and now attend his church.

From Russia came news of a Russian seaman who received a copy of the booklet in Norway. Before arriving back home in St Petersburg he had trusted Christ. On his return he shared his new faith with his wife, who also became a Christian.

At the Utah State Fair in Salt Lake City 2,100 booklets were distributed. Two ladies found one on the floor as they were walking to the fair and one of them read it out aloud to the other. They immediately understood the message of the booklet and prayed together, asking for their sins to be forgiven and putting their trust in Jesus Christ.

A Christian in Tamil Nadu, Southern India, was given a copy of the booklet and emailed John to say that it was 'well-written with an inspiring and thought-provoking message'. He wanted to give out a copy to all the non-Christian professionals where he worked, and John immediately sent him the required number of booklets.

Another email from Cape Town, South Africa, told of a man being given the booklet at a time when he had 'lost all hope of living'. The message of new life in Jesus came at just the right time and gave him hope for the future.

A message from Malaga thanked John for sending a supply of the booklet and said that these were to be used in a huge beach outreach to young people.

John was recently told of five requests from prisoners in USA and Canada who said the message of the booklet had changed their lives.

A lady from Luyengo in Swaziland bought a copy of *Ultimate Questions* because the cover attracted her. After reading it she responded to the offer of a free copy of *Read Mark Learn* so that she could do a Bible study with her neighbours. This offer has continued to be made for the past twenty-five years, with books and Bibles being sent out free of charge to every continent. This is still done by Tricia Rubens, who deals with hundreds of letters every year; there has been a particularly high response from those in prison in North America and in many parts of Africa.

In October 2010 John flew to Portugal to be one of three preachers at the FIEL (Portuguese for 'Faithful') Conference. This was held in Agua de Madeiros, a ninety- minute drive north of Lisbon. The theme of the conference was 'The Glory of God', and John shared the ministry with Luis Sayao from Brazil and the American missionary Karl Peterson, who had been serving God in South Africa and Mozambique for fifteen years. FIEL was founded by Richard Denham and his wife, a couple whose passion was to provide Christian literature in the Portuguese language. From a slow, small start, FIEL has grown over many years and now has a worldwide ministry in book publishing and on the Internet.

In January 2011 John returned to Portugal and spoke at the International Evangelical Church of the Algarve. This fellowship began in a Portuguese hotel in 1985 but in 1993 moved into a lovely purpose-built church. John's message was translated to a 'vibrant congregation' with a love for God's Word and a great concern for local evangelism and overseas missions.

A bonus for John came in the form of a Men's Breakfast at Pinheiros Altos Golf Club, which aroused so much interest that it was quickly opened up to ladies too. Over eighty people listened to John's message and many took copies of *Is Anybody out There?*

In 2011 a paperback edition of *Does God Believe in Atheists?* was published. It was revised and updated with an added bonus of including *Dealing with Dawkins* as an appendix. John received an email from Dr Richard Gibbons, Senior Pastor of First Presbyterian Church of Greenville, South Carolina:

> I have to tell you what a truly outstanding piece this is. It is masterful in its contents, brilliantly written, and the sheer creativity you have put into it is simply breathtaking. It is a delight to read and deepens my already immense regard for you. I cannot think of a greater communicator of biblical faith than you.

On 17 February 2011 John visited Epsom cemetery to mark the first anniversary of Joyce's death. A magnificent memorial stone now marks her grave, which is in a stunning position at the top of the cemetery. It reads, 'With Christ, which is far better.' John has chosen this text because 'it means that even after my body is laid there I'll be able to carry on giving my testimony'. His enormous sense of loss remains but he says that this is always overwhelmed by the complete assurance that Joyce is now in the glorious presence of her God and Saviour, Jesus Christ. He remains thankful to the countless Christian friends who uphold him in prayer, including many whom he has never met.

10
Lifting the Saviour high

In April 2011 John crossed the Atlantic for the 159th time to visit churches and friends that have become very dear to him. Howard went with him and together they visited seven states in three weeks, which included the Easter weekend. It was an emotional time for John as he met many close friends for the first time without Joyce at his side.

He preached four times in Christ Community Fellowship, Albuquerque, New Mexico, and was able to meet his good friend Pastor Bob Brown once more. The area is over 5,000 feet above sea level and this caused both John and Howard problems with breathing and sleeping. Despite this John was able to share with the congregation what he calls 'the key to salvation and probably the greatest statement in the whole Bible' in

Romans 1:17: 'The righteous will live by faith.' This is the foundational principle of the Christian life — that we live by faith and not by sight. 'We don't know how the circumstances of our lives fit into God's plan,' said John, 'and we don't need to know.' He sees a 'sad craving' in some Christian circles for signs, wonders and extra-biblical revelations.

He is greatly disturbed by the content of much of the so-called 'Christian TV' in the USA which is broadcast across the world. He said, 'I watch a little of it for my information and very little of it for my sanctification.' Shamelessly tearing Scripture out of context, televangelists passionately assure viewers that if they will 'sow a seed' to support their ministry ('… all major credit cards accepted') the donors will be guaranteed a breakthrough in their lives, delivering them from all their physical, financial and relational problems. Diseases will be healed, malignant tumours will vanish, debts will disappear and fractured relationships will be healed. Claims like these are aired twenty-four hours a day. 'Yet,' said John, 'Jesus did not shed his blood to guarantee that his followers get the best jobs, or to boost their bank balances, or to keep them in perfect physical condition. He died to deliver his people from the penalty and power of sin, and after death from its very presence.'

One of the most helpful chapters in the Bible, as far as John is concerned, is the account of Paul's 'thorn in the flesh' (2 Corinthians 12). Paul's testimony was not that he had been healed. It was much better than that. He was given a promise from God: 'My grace is sufficient for you.' It is a natural desire for us to want instant deliverance from trials, traumas and illnesses. But John continued, 'Hear me carefully, faith has another option,' and he read out a statement made by Joni Eareckson Tada, who dived into the waters of Chesapeake Bay as a teenager in 1967 and came out totally paralysed from the neck down. Over forty years later she said:

> When we learn to lean back on God's sovereignty, fixing and settling our thoughts on that unshakeable, unmoveable reality, we can experience great inner peace. Our troubles may not change. Our pain may not diminish. Our loss may not be restored. Our problems may not fade with the new dawn, but the power of those things to harm us is broken as we rest on the fact that God is in control.

John also recalled meeting the legendary Baptist pastor affectionately known as 'Preacher Hallock' in Oklahoma in 2001. John was due to share a platform with him and had been looking forward to this for some time. However, on his arrival he discovered that the pastor was seriously ill and not expected to live much longer. John asked whether it would be appropriate to visit him, and this was arranged. The great man was now small, very frail and in constant pain. John simply sat on the floor at his feet and listened as the pastor told him how he had prayed for healing but God had given him something more valuable. He had given him the 'ministry of suffering' and in this he had found the full meaning of the promise that God's grace is sufficient. This moved John beyond words and it is an experience he will never forget.

John believes and worships a God who is 'able to heal every sickness and disease in every person on this planet. But there is another option — that we fix our eyes on God's wisdom and sovereignty and learn to accept his dealings with us and trust him regardless of what those dealings are.' That is what John has chosen to do, and he can testify to God's absolute trustworthiness and the sufficiency of his grace.

John once heard the Minor Prophets referred to as the Bible's 'clean pages' because they are not often read. He preached twice from these 'clean pages' before leaving Albuquerque. On the first occasion he spoke about Habakkuk and started by remarking on the difference between the American and British pronunciation of the prophet's name. 'But you are wrong', he said. 'Any country that parks on the driveway and drives on the parkway has clearly no idea how to pronounce Habakkuk correctly!' From this book John showed the importance of God's ultimate word to Habakkuk: 'The righteous will live by his faith' (Habakkuk 2:4). This tells us that nothing — not even the most calamitous of national or international developments — must be allowed to shake our utter confidence in the settled sovereignty of God.

On the second occasion he chose Jonah who, he said, committed the most daring act of disobedience in the Bible apart from Adam and Eve. Jonah could not accept God's sovereignty or understand why God would act in the way he did. Yet the sovereignty of God is one of the most liberating doctrines in the whole of Scripture. It means that all his ways are perfect, even when they don't fit into our agendas, our denominational boxes and our theological pigeonholes. John told a story of two young boys from a tiny village who met one day and started chatting. They discovered they both went to church but one was puzzled why he hadn't seen the other boy in church. 'That's because you belong to a different abomination to me,' said the boy. John reminded his listeners that God is not limited by anything we create and that the gospel is for all men everywhere, regardless of their lifestyles and behaviour, including those whose lifestyles offend us. Jonah abandoned God, but God did not abandon Jonah. God goes to any lengths to bring about his sovereign purposes and to bless his people. In Jonah's case this meant being swallowed by a great fish. 'Fortunately,' said John, 'the fish believed in small prophets and quick returns!' Jonah survived the ordeal and was re-commissioned, which reassures us that nobody is too bad for God to restore and bless.

John then preached at First Presbyterian Church, Jackson, Mississippi, and was sorry to miss his good friend Dr Ligon Duncan, who was attending a conference elsewhere, but was very pleased to stay once more with Dr Bill and Mrs Lou Anne Harper. Here John and Howard experienced severe weather extremes and narrowly missed a tornado with winds of up to 135 mph which wrecked cars on a road they had travelled down only an hour before. On the drive to Birmingham, Alabama, they drove through Tuscaloosa, which soon afterwards was hit by the worst system of tornados to strike the country for almost forty years.

John preached at Briarwood Presbyterian Church, where Pastor Harry Reeder heads a staff of 200 and has 30,000 events in any one year. He attended a breakfast at a Cracker Barrel restaurant where he faced questions from a razor-sharp class of seminary students. Afterwards he declared himself to be 'usefully stretched' in discussing theological and practical issues.

John's sermons were aired on local radio and in one sermon he recalled being in Dallas, Texas, on 9 November 1989 and switching the television on to watch the news with Joyce. They could not understand why the major news item simply showed people knocking down a wall. But this was no ordinary wall; it was the Berlin Wall, and this was a truly electrifying moment that set millions free. Yet this is nothing compared to the ultimate global moment when Jesus Christ will return to this earth. If that happens in John's lifetime his ministry will be over. There will be no atheists, no agnostics, sceptics or doubters. That includes Joseph Stalin, Pol Pot, Mao Tse-Tung, Adolf Hitler and Saddam Hussein, who 'will experience the dreadful reality that hell is truth seen too late'. The Bible tells us that everyone will admit that Jesus Christ is Lord, including today's atheists such as Richard Dawkins. 'I hope they do it before that moment,' said John, 'but if they don't do it now, they will do it then.'

John also spoke about repentance — what he called a missing note in many areas of the Christian church today. He said the entire Christian life should be one of repentance because the Christian who has stopped repenting has stopped growing. It is no good professing Christians in our churches clapping their hands when they should be wringing them, or leaping in the air when they should be falling to their knees. He issued a passionate challenge asking, 'Where is the call to repentance? Where is the sorrow for sin?' Then he spoke to anyone present who was not a Christian and urged them to turn away from their sin, to abandon everything they trusted in, as he had done when a young man, and to fling themselves on Jesus Christ and trust him as their personal Saviour. He quoted David Dickson, the Scottish divine, who said, 'I took my bad deeds and threw them on a heap; then I took my good deeds and flung them on the same heap.' 'The time to do that', said John, 'is now.'

At the invitation of another long-time friend, Trey Lee, John and Howard visited The Reserve at Lake Keowee, South Carolina, which is an award-winning community in the foothills of the Blue Ridge Mountains. It is known as 'an exceptional and timeless place', and both John and Howard found this to be so. The two keen golfers were able to play on its championship golf course designed by Jack Nicklaus — which went some way towards overcoming the deep disappointment of not being able to get tickets to the US Masters while they were in Augusta! When John went into the club-house he was shown to a locker with his own name engraved on a brass plate and told that he was now an honorary member of the club. Only golfers will under-stand the enormity of this gesture. John was deeply touched and overwhelmed by this and for once in his life he was speechless. This was followed by an evening dinner at the club held in his honour, at which several guests spoke of how God had used his ministry to impact on their lives. Trey read out a letter from his mother saying how much Joyce had meant to her and there were many tears. It was a deeply moving occasion and John closed the evening with an impromptu epilogue.

On Easter Day John and Howard were in Grand Blanc, Michigan, to share fellowship with another dear friend, Pastor Bob Dickie at Berean Baptist Church. The morning began with a Sunrise Service held in a mausoleum in Crestwood Memorial Cemetery. Surrounded by hundreds of occupied graves, the assembled folk were able to celebrate an empty grave and a risen, living Saviour. This was followed by breakfast in the church and a triumphant morning service. John spoke about the frightened disciples, hiding away in fear after the crucifixion Yet a few days later they burst out of their hideout and onto the streets of Jerusalem shouting for joy that Jesus was alive. They didn't care whether they were arrested, tortured or put to death. They were changed men because they had seen the risen Jesus. John went on:

> Hear me carefully, people are sometimes willing to lay down their lives for something they believe to be true (the 9/11 terrorists did that) but nobody

is prepared to give his life for something he knows to be false. The disciples were transformed from frightened rabbits to roaring lions because of the resurrection of Jesus Christ.

John's challenging and encouraging ministry was put on the church website and a large number of people listened and downloaded the talks.

There is no let-up after a hectic tour and at Boston Airport, while waiting for the flight home, John had already engaged Howard in forward planning!

John preached a little closer to home, at Banstead Community Church, on Whit Sunday. He spoke about the first Day of Pentecost, when the Holy Spirit was given to the disciples. John was careful to explain the difference between receiving the Holy Spirit when a person becomes a Christian and then seeking to be continually filled as a means of spiritual growth from then on. This is an ongoing process, and not some exotic, dramatic experience. It has three results: Jesus is glorified, the church is edified and the Christian is sanctified.

It saddens John when he sees so many Christians on what he calls 'cruise control', rather than hungering and thirsting after righteousness. He suggested that his listeners should ask themselves two questions: 'Do I really want to have done with all my sins? Do I long to be holy in thought, word and action?' He recalled hearing about a farmer who started to hold Bible studies in his home. He could accommodate twenty people, and no more. When asked a few months later how things were going he said the house was now full, with thirty people every week. He explained that he had thrown out a large, unused sideboard and this had made the extra room. A few weeks later he had forty people in his house because he had thrown out another piece of old furniture to make more room. John emphasized that the Christian already has the Holy Spirit living within but there needs to be a continuous cleaning out of 'old furniture' and a willingness to put away anything and everything that would prevent it. John preaches from his heart and from personal experience. He does not ask his listeners to do something he does not do himself.

He concluded by saying that the secret of being filled is to keep on drinking. He issued an invitation: keep coming to the Bible, determined to listen to God's voice, to heed his warnings, to obey his commands, to follow his leading and to live holy, God-honouring lives.

During this busy year John had medical tests and investigations which are ongoing, but this did not prevent him from having a full diary. In September he went to the Festival della Letteratura in Italy. This is a huge secular annual book fair to which 110,000 come from all over the world. The church Sola Grazia organized a five-day outreach and asked John to speak on atheism and on 'Where was God on September 11th?' because this was the tenth anniversary of 9/11. A New York policeman, a Christian who was on duty at Ground Zero, also attended and gave his personal testimony. Churches in the Bologna area were excited to meet John at last, having used *Ultimate Questions* and *Why believe the Bible?* for a long time as their evangelistic tools. All the churches appreciated his making the journey to visit them and were greatly encouraged by his visit and the clear presentation of the gospel.

When John was a small boy on Guernsey his father's hobby was repairing and cleaning watches. Many times John watched him take the back off a watch to reveal tiny cogs, wheels and sprockets. Some were moving one way slowly, while others were going the other way quickly. To the little boy it looked utterly confusing and made no sense at all. But when his father turned the watch over he saw that all the contradictory movements were combining to move the hands in the right direction and in perfect time. John often thinks about that. At times our world looks to be in utter confusion and we wonder what is going on. But he says that when we get to heaven we shall see that God was working all the time to bring about his unchanging and perfect purposes. Even today, when the enemy seems to be achieving so much, he is only accomplishing that which God is allowing and bringing under subjection to his eternal will.

2012 is a 'milestone year' for John as he celebrates fifty years in full-time Christian ministry and also, unbelievably, his eightieth birthday. In addition it marks the thirty-year relationship between John and his publishers, EP, and the twenty-fifth anniversary of the publication of *Ultimate Questions*. The year is already mapped out with PCAP tours, visits to Italy and Albania and another preaching tour in the USA. The Christian Television Association is making a second documentary about his life, to include footage of John in Guernsey, the UK (including Islay), Albania and the USA. This year also sees the publication of his new book *Major points from the Minor Prophets*, which is a result of his studies in the Bible's 'clean pages'. He hopes the book will encourage a greater enthusiasm for the life-changing truths to be found within them. This is yet another addition to the long list of invaluable publications which are his legacy to the world.

John says an athlete does not slow down when he sees the finishing line; he runs with renewed effort. With God's gracious help, John continues to lift the Saviour high and renews his efforts daily. This is his story to date, but who knows what God still has in store? Through the past fifty years countless numbers of people all over the world have heard John speak about the good news of the gospel of Jesus Christ. But, as he frequently says, hearing is not enough. After preaching on one occasion Rev. John Stott was approached by a member of the congregation who thanked him and said, 'I have learned an enormous amount from you today.' Stott replied, 'Then tell me what you will do with it.'

When John spoke at Berean Baptist Church in Grand Blanc, Michigan, on Easter Sunday 2011 he shared with them the words he had written on the floral wreath he placed on Joyce's grave: 'In loving and grateful memory of my darling wife Joyce, until by the grace of our God and Saviour Jesus Christ we meet again in heaven.' It was a deeply personal moment. In the silence that followed he looked round the church and quietly asked, 'Will I meet you in heaven? Will you be there? The only way is if you have put your trust in Jesus Christ as your Lord and Saviour.'

John speaks with great certainty and from personal experience of a daily relationship with Jesus Christ, in whom he placed his complete trust over fifty years ago. He has seen unprecedented changes in his lifetime and has experienced trauma and sadness as well as excitement and happiness. Throughout it all his faith has remained rock-solid, his message has not changed and his destination is assured. He continues to defend

Christianity fiercely and his life is an ongoing testimony to the living reality and faithfulness of its founder.

You have learned an enormous amount about John in this book, but that is not enough. Neither is that its primary purpose. Most importantly, you have learned the truth about the Lord Jesus Christ and your need to turn to him in repentance and faith.

Hear me carefully — what will you do with it?